T0115444

Praise for
Meet the Frugalwoods

"*Meet the Frugalwoods* offers an accessible, thoughtful, and transformative philosophy of intentional financial living. Liz shares her journey of finding financial freedom on her own terms—inspiring us to challenge our own ideas of achievement and our expectations around how we should be living as we work toward it."—Stefanie O'Connell, author of *The Broke and Beautiful Life*

"I defy anyone to read *Meet the Frugalwoods* without a highlighter in hand, taking notes and starting in-depth conversations with their loved ones. This is the memoir-focused approach to finance everyone's been waiting for, especially those who could never get all the way through a money book before." —Erin Lowry, author of *Broke Millennial: Stop Scraping by and Get Your Financial Life Together*

"Forget any of the preconceived beliefs you might have about what it means to be frugal. In *Meet the Frugalwoods*, Liz shows us it is about so much more than saving money. You will finish the book questioning what you're working toward, and feel inspired to take action so you can live a more meaningful life."—Cait Flanders, author of *The Year of Less*

"A remarkable and inspirational journey, not of deprivation but of joy, contentment, spirituality, and, of course, financial independence. Along the way you'll be inspired, and you just might see a new path for yourself."—JL Collins, author of *The Simple Path to Wealth*

"Get ready to have your life changed forever: *Meet the Frugalwoods* is a political, self-help, personal finance, and environmental manifesto set to be a new classic for building a meaningful and sustainable life, community, and society." —Emma Johnson, author of the bestselling *The Kickass Single Mom*

MEET THE FRUGALWOODS

Meet the
FRUGALWOODS

Achieving Financial Independence Through Simple Living

ELIZABETH WILLARD THAMES

HARPER
BUSINESS

An Imprint of HarperCollins*Publishers*

This is not designed to be a definitive guide to finance nor am I a professional financial planner. Given the risk involved in investing of almost any kind there is no guarantee that any investment method in this book will be profitable. Neither I nor my publisher can assume the liability that comes with the risk in applying the methods described in this book, and any such liability is hereby expressly disclaimed.

MEET THE FRUGALWOODS. Copyright © 2018 by Elizabeth Willard Thames. All rights reserved. Printed in the United States of America. No part of this book may be used or reproduced in any manner whatsoever without written permission except in the case of brief quotations embodied in critical articles and reviews. For information, address HarperCollins Publishers, 195 Broadway, New York, NY 10007.

HarperCollins books may be purchased for educational, business, or sales promotional use. For information, please email the Special Markets Department at SPsales@harpercollins.com.

FIRST HARPER BUSINESS PAPERBACK EDITION PUBLISHED 2019

A hardcover edition of this book was published in 2018 by Harper Business, an imprint of HarperCollins Publishers.

Designed by Bonni Leon-Berman

Library of Congress Cataloging-in-Publication Data has been applied for.

ISBN 978-0-06-266814-1 (pbk.)

22 23   LSC   10 9 8 7 6 5 4 3 2

To women everywhere who don't think they can manage their money, who aren't confident in their skills, and who underestimate their own worth and intelligence. You are far smarter, far more capable, and far worthier than you realize.

CONTENTS

INTRODUCTION

As I write this, I'm sitting on the back porch of the rural Vermont homestead I share with my husband and our daughter, gazing out on the sixty-six acres of forest, fruit trees, gardens, ponds, and streams that we feel incredibly lucky to call our own. Just a few years ago, this seemed like an impossible feat. My husband and I were struggling to conceive a baby and attempting to chart a path out of our frenzied nine-to-five grind in urban Cambridge, Massachusetts. We wanted to achieve financial independence, quit the cubicle jobs that made us so unhappy, and create a simpler life of purpose in a rural setting.

This is the story of how we brought that dream to fruition before our thirty-third birthdays. My husband, Nate, and I are not exceptional people. We're not rich or famous or geniuses or even particularly good-looking (although we have our moments). We're just some average, middle-class kids from the Midwest who decided we wanted something more out of life than what our consumer culture sells us. We realized we couldn't buy our way to happiness and that we had to restructure how we lived, what we spent our money on, and how we used our time in order to achieve deep fulfillment and lasting contentment.

I've heard people say things along the lines of "anyone

can achieve financial independence" and "people are poor because they don't work hard enough" and "my success stems entirely from my own efforts" and I disagree with all of those sentiments. While it's true that Nate and I are average people, and we've never won the lottery or had investment banker salaries or been the beneficiaries of inheritances or trust funds, I'm keenly aware that we are also extraordinarily privileged.

Poverty is a pervasive issue, not only in our country but globally, and it's myopic to presume that everyone who is poor doesn't work hard enough or isn't motivated enough. It's often quite the contrary. Many people who live at or below the poverty line work much harder than I ever have or probably ever will. Working two and three jobs in an effort to simply pay rent and buy groceries and send their kids to school in shoes that fit is the punishing reality for many people. Frugality is often already a requirement for those at the lowest end of the economic spectrum and there's simply not enough money coming in every month to save enough to create a stable financial base, let alone an emergency fund or retirement savings or investments. In order to save large amounts of money, you have to have a sufficient amount of money coming in. You can't frugalize income you don't earn.

Without an emergency fund, a savings account, or any type of financial cushion, people who live paycheck to paycheck are in a perilous position. One missed shift can equal a missed rent payment or a missed electricity bill. Compounding this problem is the fact that many economically disadvantaged people lack a bank account, which means they're unable to take advantage of the lending opportunities or overdraft protections that a large financial services firm can provide.

It's my belief that we, as a country, need a stronger social safety net for the working poor. We need comprehensive medical and dental coverage, we need welfare programs that don't strand families who earn just barely too much money to qualify for housing and food subsidies, we need to care not only for our children and our elderly, but also for adults who struggle—for any number of reasons—to cobble together a livable wage. I'm a proponent of exploring a universal basic income, as studies have demonstrated that entrusting people with money of their own often yields tremendous dividends for society as a whole. No one wins when a family has to choose between working a job or safe childcare. No one wins when the only food options in a neighborhood are unhealthy and expensive. No one wins when people are forced to use the emergency room as their primary care physician. As a nation and as a society, I believe we have a responsibility to care for those who experience the greatest need and to create viable pathways out of generational poverty.

I share all of this with you because it's easy when talking about one's personal journey—which is what this book is—to extrapolate and make the assumption that if only everyone did as we did, then they too would experience success. But that's not the case. It's naive, presumptuous, and grossly lacking in empathy to assume as much.

In many ways, my privilege and my husband's privilege took root in our lives long before we were even born. Both of our parents had college educations, had good careers, owned homes, and were in happy, financially stable marriages before we were even conceived. These factors all combined to mean that by the time we were born, Nate and I were already several steps ahead of many of the other babies in the hospital that day. Adding to the circumstances of our families is the fact that we were born into safe, middle-class neighborhoods in the United States and thus were the beneficiaries of excellent medical care, superb public schools, plenty of nutritious foods, vibrant public library systems, summer camps, girl/boy scout troops, church communities, horseback riding lessons, ballet classes, basketball teams, and much more.

All of these privileges wove themselves together to form the basis for happy, warm, well-educated, well-cared-for childhoods. We didn't suffer traumas as children. We didn't endure domestic violence. We never experienced food insecurity. We were never homeless. Our electricity and water were never turned off. We were never evicted. We weren't exposed to parental drug use or addiction. Rather, we were encouraged, taught to read at home, taken on family trips to art museums and the symphony, shown how to cook and clean, disciplined with fair but firm methodology, taught to play nicely with our siblings, given pets to care for, and above all, loved unconditionally.

These factors are profound in charting a person's course through life and all of these benefits of our upbringings contributed in large part to the successes we've enjoyed as adults. And our privilege doesn't stop there. My husband and I are both white and heterosexual. I wish I didn't have to include these two facts as "privileges" because I believe that people of all races, religions, genders, ethnicities, backgrounds, and sexual orientations should be treated equally. Sadly, however, that isn't the case in our country and so I have to include these as factors integral to our successes. I wasn't subjected to individual or institutional biases in my applications for college, for graduate school, or for jobs. I was able to succeed in both academics and my career without the strain of racism or homophobia or any number of other prejudices.

While I do think there are elements of my journey through extreme frugality that could be useful to anyone, I also realize that my frugality is elective. I don't *have* to save as much money as I do. I'm not pinching pennies in order to eat. I'm not a missed paycheck away from bankruptcy. I choose to be frugal and I choose to live a lifestyle that has granted me financial independence. But it's no more due to my own aptitude than the fact that I can read and write.

Sure, I had to work hard to learn to read and write, but I also had parents and teachers helping me out at every turn. I wish I could say that if everyone followed my advice, they too could reach financial independence, but that's simply not the case. There are too many layers of institutional privilege enabling my story for it to be replicable for everyone.

There are many people who transcend difficult childhoods to achieve at the highest levels. Who you will grow up to be isn't imprinted at birth or predetermined by who your parents are. But it's undeniable that the road was easier for me. I didn't have to overcome anything in order to get where I am today. A memoir can only honestly represent a person's lived experiences, which is why I felt it was important to share all of the ways in which privilege courses through my life.

I wrote this book to tell the story of how Nate and I did the unexpected. Of how we broke free. I also want to encourage you to ask yourself the questions that guided our journey: What would you do if you didn't need your paycheck? What's your passion in life? And what's stopping you from making that a reality? I fully recognize that having the ability to even ask ourselves these questions is profoundly privileged. For many people, questions like these are wholly out of reach and divorced from their daily slog of trying to make ends meet.

What are you doing that you love? That you hate? How do you use your time and money? And how do you *wish* you used your time and money? Bringing your hopes into alignment with your actions is my boldest edict. Too often, we're slotted into predetermined roles by societal expectations, family pressures, and, in my case, our own internal conception of what our lives "should" look like. When we're able to stop the cycle of impressing others and spending money in an effort to assuage the frustrations we feel, true liberation can take hold in our lives. Identifying whether every dollar we spend is for a need or a want enables us to craft a life that's focused on living out our priorities—not the priorities of anyone else or of society at large—but the priorities that matter most to us. In the pages that follow, I hope you find inspiration and motivation to pursue your best life.

MEET THE FRUGALWOODS

1

College Grad Seeks Meaningful, Gainful Employment. Fails.

I needed a job because I needed money to pay rent, a position most people find themselves in at some point in time. More than that, I wanted to climb on to what I saw as the first rung of adulthood: a career-track job that you got business cards for and had to wear a suit to. I wanted to be taken seriously. I was obsessed with doing what I thought I *should* do because, up to this point, it'd worked out pretty well for me.

Sitting on a molded plastic chair in the temp agency office, I took the first job they offered me: working in a single-story beige warehouse Monday through Friday from 7 a.m. to 3 p.m., preparing documents for digitization. This wasn't anywhere near what I'd envisioned and I was pretty sure I didn't need to wear a suit. But I also didn't want to waste time waiting for someone to call me back about my apparently worthless résumé. If nothing else was going to pan out for me, I figured I might as well earn some money.

It was June 2006 and I was twenty-two years old. I'd graduated with honors from the University of Kansas the month before, feeling flush with accomplishment. Since my freshman year of high school, that'd been my goal, and I'd assumed that was all I needed to do in order to ensure lifelong success. The formula for life, as I understood it, was: you go to college, you get good grades, you graduate, you get a good job, and you live happily ever after, right?!

Somehow, that wasn't working out. I was a rule follower, a syllabus and spreadsheet lover, but now, I was adrift without a rubric. I'd written what I thought was a very nice résumé and cover letter and sent it in response to no fewer than fifty-three different job openings located all over the country at nonprofits ranging from art museums to soup kitchens, all of which I figured would welcome a liberal arts major like myself with open arms. Not a single one called me back. Or emailed me back. Or even let me know they'd so much as *received* my application. I was throwing myself against the doors of adulthood, equipped with everything I'd been taught to bring to this stage of life, and no one was answering.

Every day I worked at that beige, one-story warehouse was a carbon copy of the day before: I opened a dusty, green, legal-size file folder, took out the top piece of paper, and pressed it down on the table under my palms, spreading from the center outward, my hands flattening each corner as I went. Next I checked for staples, which I'd remove like unwanted teeth with a sadistic rip from the metal jaws of my staple remover, heedless of the gaping maw left in its wake. I peeled off Post-it notes so old they barely posted anymore, and taped them down on all four sides to a blank piece of paper I'd whisk up with my rubber-covered fingertip from a stack in the center of the table. I'd then pick up the second piece of paper from the folder and begin afresh, as if for the first time, until I'd performed this ritual on every single piece of paper in the folder. Then I'd move on to the next folder in my in-box.

I sat on a metal folding chair at a plastic folding table with two other women in this windowless, cavernous warehouse. I was just five miles from where I'd blissfully spent the past four years double majoring in political science and creative writing, which I'd assumed would somehow alchemize into a profession. I'd never quite identified what that profession might be, but I figured that applying for jobs would be like applying for college: line up all the correct paperwork, check all the right boxes, and get accepted. That's adulthood, right?!

The warehouse had gray-painted concrete walls and I couldn't figure out why you'd bother to paint concrete gray, something I had plenty of time to mull over because there was no variation to my days, no additional tasks, nothing to do but get a box of files every morning and sit at my table for eight hours, straightening edges. The two women who worked alongside me were nice enough, and we'd chat as we worked or I'd listen to NPR on my headphones. I was sinking into depression and what I can honestly say was ennui: Was this why I'd gotten a BA? Why I'd pulled all-nighters for four years to eke out a 4.0? I felt like I was spiraling downward into an abyss that would terminate with me living in my parents' basement, which wasn't even finished, and babysitting their neighbor's kids. (See? Ennui.) To me at twenty-two, that sounded like about the worst thing that could happen to a person. I hadn't even lived at my parents' house during summers since my freshman year. I wanted, more than anything, to be an independent person. A person who could find a job.

Adding to my embarrassment and frustration over my failure to launch was the fact that my closest confidant, my boyfriend, Nate, was hired for a real job (a job with a salary, that one might list on a résumé, and that one wouldn't be mortified to admit one did) before we even graduated. I'd been a better student than Nate, with more As and more extracurriculars, so I seethed with jealousy. He had an internship all of our senior year, which he'd spent more time at than he had studying, and then they'd offered him a full-time position. My internship at the city arts center, conversely, had not translated into a job, even though I'd applied for their entry-level administrative assistant position. I'd spent more time studying, a strategy I was starting to question now that I was so raw with envy as I toiled in a warehouse at a plastic folding table. I felt duped. No one had warned me about this postgraduate purgatory of being educated but inexperienced and unqualified to do, well, really anything.

Sitting in my 1990 light blue Toyota Camry station wagon in the parking lot of the document scanning warehouse in late July, I had my cell phone clamped to my ear and I thought I was going to sweat to death. The air conditioning in the car—which I'd paid cash for myself at age sixteen, with money saved up from my babysitting and church receptionist gigs—didn't work. The only way to stay cool was to run the fan on the highest setting. But the problem was that between the engine and the fan, I couldn't hear my potential future boss on the line, sitting as she was in her office on the twenty-sixth floor of a building in midtown Manhattan, which I imagined to be sleek, snowy white, and generously air-conditioned. I'd had the car door open to allow in some hot Kansas breeze, but then I could hear my colleagues who were also on break chatting and laughing from the warehouse steps, oblivious to my potentially life-changing phone conversation over here. I waved to them so that if I passed out and didn't come back into work, someone would find me before I roasted. I wedged a notebook between the steering wheel and my stomach and tried to take notes without smearing the ink with my sweat. I made a mental note to sit on the passenger side for any and all future phone interviews. This was my third call with AmeriCorps, and it sounded like they might be as desperate to hire someone as I was to be hired.

Nate's job was in Kansas City so I'd started my search there, thinking we could live together. Although in all honesty, I wasn't thinking we'd just *live* together; I was thinking we'd get engaged and *then* live together. I wanted everything adultlike to happen immediately: career, marriage, kids, house, and a dog too, come to think of it. I brought this up with Nate in what I considered a casual, wondering-what-you're-thinking-about-us-and-marriage sort of way, which always seems to come off as aggressive and gauche when I try to do it. Due to my enduring lack of suavity, Nate knew exactly what I was driving at and flat out told me he didn't want to get engaged until after we'd had some time in the real world. Some experience beyond our collegiate bubble that provided everything we needed: structure, purpose, a social life, beer. In retaliation for his mature coolheadedness, I veered my job search to the East Coast, since that seemed like a good way to show Nate how miserable his life would be without me.

After two months of fruitless searching I came across AmeriCorps, which didn't pay a salary per se, but which did provide what seemed like worthy résumé fodder. At the very least, I figured it was several steps up from document-scanning doom in a warehouse in suburban Kansas, which is a pretty low bar to step over. Turns out, AmeriCorps wanted me. Offer letter in hand, I quit my document-scanning gig in what I imagined to be a triumphant flourish (although no one seemed to notice). It was late August and I retreated to my parents' two-story brick subdivision home in suburban—*far* suburban—St. Louis, Missouri, to prepare for my decampment to the exotic-sounding New York City.

Later that week, I stood in the fluorescent-lit dressing room of the JCPenney at the West County mall wearing a size four, shoulder-padded, gray plaid skirt suit with pink piping and a pink top peeking out from underneath the jacket. My mom said it looked very professional, and since she and my dad offered to buy me, in her words, "a career wardrobe" as a graduation present, I agreed. This was a job in an office, after all, which I assumed meant wearing a suit and nylons every day. Equipped with five suits and two pairs of the only low heels that fit me—Naturalizer pumps, a brand patronized primarily by women my mother's age—unengaged, and having never set (long, narrow) foot in New York City before in all my twenty-two years, I got on a plane bound for LaGuardia with the maximum allowable baggage.

As my taxi from the airport pulled up to a rundown, graffiti-covered, three-story walk-up in pre-gentrified Crown Heights, Brooklyn, conveniently located across the street from a blocks-long abandoned warehouse with not a single intact pane in its windows, I asked the driver to double-check the address, because there was no way this was my apartment. But he wasn't wrong. This was, according to his map and the address I'd written down, where I now lived.

My roommates—two of my friends from college who also had offer letters for New York City–based jobs—had picked this place out, and to be fair, the only requirement I'd given them was "cheap." I'd gotten on a plane in the suburban, safe, middle-class—I'd previously said "bland," but bland was sounding pretty good right about now—Midwest and landed in one of the more notorious neighborhoods of urban, intimidating (to me, anyway), working-class Brooklyn.

As I climbed the stairs to my apartment with my suitcases digging into my palms and slamming against my legs, I hoped Nate was missing me in a painful, longing, I-should-have-proposed sort of way, because this had better be worth it. Unpacking didn't take much time since there was a firm ceiling on how much I could cram into two suitcases and two carry-ons. AmeriCorps would pay me $10,000 for the year, and I had a few hundred dollars in the bank that I'd saved up from my various college jobs as a writing tutor, a money counter at the Six Flags theme park, a hostess at the Olive Garden, a receptionist at a car dealership, and a camp counselor. AmeriCorps tactfully referred to my $10,000, an amount too small to legally be called a salary, as a "service stipend."

The idea behind AmeriCorps is that youths (like me) work at small nonprofits in impoverished communities for a year and, in return, gain valuable job experience. I would sound much more altruistic if I said I chose AmeriCorps because I wanted to give back—and that was part of it—but more crucially? Nowhere else would hire me. I was determined to live on this $10,000 stipend because I didn't have any debt whatsoever. My parents helped me pay for college, plus I'd had scholarships, plus I'd worked, plus KU was very cheap, and I wasn't about to take on debt in this first test of adulthood. Given this budget, there was no way I could afford furniture, so I decided to build it out of cardboard boxes. Not furniture that came packed in cardboard boxes, but out of the cardboard itself. I cut banana boxes, stacked them, and taped them together to make a sort of dresser with open shelves. Next, I turned a box upside-down and put a sheet over it as a tablecloth. Voilà! A bedside table. I rolled out my yoga mat on the floor of my windowless bedroom and covered it with the pillow and blanket I'd stuffed into one of my suitcases. I was triumphant. I felt industrious and independent, like a modern-day Virginia Woolf striking out on my own, unbeholden to parents or boyfriend for funds and able to craft a room of one's own from cardboard. I figured if I could make my own free furniture, I could probably hack it as an adult. I'll admit that the yoga-mat-as-bed did get old after a week, so I saved up to buy the cheapest mattress (plus delivery) that I could find at the Atlantic Center Mall in Brooklyn. There were limits to my thriftiness. I bought a "map of the world" shower curtain because I hate wasting time and figured that bathing and brushing teeth could be made into multitasking opportunities to enhance one's knowledge of geography. That is how I learned that the Seychelles are a thing, so clearly, I needed this map. And with that, I was moved in.

Walking down Franklin Avenue, my new street, I saw the ornate architecture underlying now-derelict buildings. I could tell that these had once been elegant brick-front row houses with curling spirals of wrought iron, expansive front steps, and square, tidy gardens out front. Now, they were chopped into warrenlike apartments fronted by patches of dirt littered with cans, newspapers, broken glass, and cigarette butts. There was an empty lot a block up from my apartment, choked with weeds and bags of garbage. Laundromats, bodegas, an off-brand dollar store, hair salons, storefront churches, and payday loan businesses were what the neighborhood offered. Graffiti coated everything, even the metal grates that shop owners pulled down to protect their glass storefronts every night. There were no restaurants or banks or gyms or coffee shops or clothing stores or grocery stores or doctor's offices. But there were people everywhere: out on stoops, chatting, calling to one another, laughing, scolding kids who ran around barefoot, seemingly oblivious to the broken glass and trash. People pushed rattling shopping carts full of cans and bottles down the center of the street, destined for the promise of five-cent returns at the neighborhood recycling center.

The Franklin Avenue subway stop, which boasted both

the 2/3 and 4/5 trains, was eight blocks from my apartment. I hustled there my first morning of work. I was so tense about messing up my train route that I barely had time to register the nuances of the street I was walking down. Those realizations would come later. After parochially jabbing my subway pass at the turnstile a few times, I stood back, watched the experienced masses streaming past, and tried to mimic the way they slid their cards through the reader. They performed this ceremony so quickly that the mechanics were almost imperceptible. It took me a good three minutes to get through, during which time I thought the throng behind me might pick me up and throw me over the turnstile. My only experience with public transit before that morning was riding on the train that went around our zoo as a kid.

I clutched my handwritten directions (this being the pre-smartphone era) in my sweaty hands, trying to keep track of which stop we were at each time the train lurched into a station. When I first got on, I'd positioned myself so that I was staring at the map above the door, which had Christmas-tree-light-size bulbs that lit up at the appropriate station. But after thirty minutes underground, there were so many people jammed into the car that I couldn't see the map anymore, and was frantically trying to make out the garbled name the conductor rattled off at each station. Everyone else seemed to know by instinct where we were. I watched it happen over and over again as people, zoning out on headphones, reading books, or flat-out asleep, would animate like wind-up toys and scurry off at their stop. I decided after forty-five minutes that I should be there by now, so I got out and realized that the names of the stations are on the walls outside the train windows, and that I'd gotten off a stop too early.

I jumped on the next train and disembarked at the correct stop this time: Grand Central Terminal in the heart of midtown Manhattan. Since most of the train population emptied out at Grand Central, I was now moving in the center of a pack of people, all shuffling up the stairs. I couldn't have turned around, or bent down, or scratched my nose without disrupting the herd of humanity I was part of. At the top of the stairs, I was spat out into Grand Central, which was the polar opposite of where I'd started my morning, with its vaulted ceilings, marble columns, and antique clocks. Investment bankers pushed past me wearing Rolex watches, and executives in red-soled Louboutins clicked around me, demonstrably annoyed that I was a stationary beacon in this otherwise constantly flowing crowd, all determined, all in a rush, all giving off a sense of purpose. Between the people and the building, I'd never seen so much wealth on display in one place. I'd also never seen so many exits in one place. From where I was standing, there appeared to be about ten, all going in different directions, with indecipherable indications of where they led. The directions I'd scribbled did not include which exit to take, so I guessed and ended up walking in roughly the direction of my new office. It was 8:40 a.m. and I was supposed to be there by nine, so I thought my timing was perfect because I needed to go into a lobby bathroom and change my shoes, brush my hair, apply lipstick, dab the stress sweat off my blouse, and top up on deodorant. When I got to my office building, however, I learned a universal New York City truth: there are no public restrooms in office buildings. Worse still, my boss, who turned out to be a poised, young, glamorous New Yorker, was standing in the lobby (in heels, without nylons) waiting for me. I walked into my first day of my first real job wearing tennis shoes over nylons, with matted hair, and with sweat dripping down my back underneath my pastel, shoulder-padded suit that would've looked perfect on a fifty-year-old midwestern real estate agent trying to sell a suburban split-level with green carpeting and a porch she insisted on referring to as the "lanai."

2

My Year of Food Stamps and Billionaires

I never thought about money a whole lot before moving to New York City. At least, not in the how-am-I-going-to-afford-to-eat sort of way. My parents aren't wealthy, but they've always owned their own home and packed school lunches with carrots and whole-wheat sandwiches for their three kids. When I was twelve, we went to Washington, DC, because my dad had a conference there and the hotel room was paid for by his work. We visited all of the free Smithsonian museums and I ate a Reuben sandwich for the first time at a restaurant near the theater where Lincoln was shot. I had no firsthand frames of reference for the outlandish wealth or the desperate poverty that New York City encompasses. Growing up, my family and I volunteered regularly at soup kitchens and donated to homeless shelters, but there's a remove when you drive an hour home afterward to the scrubbed, mono-economic suburbs. I knew intellectually that a vast chasm exists between rich and poor, but I hadn't encountered an academic or journalistic rendering of the divide that adequately conveyed the visceral feelings of experiencing it for myself. Turns out, AmeriCorps was my year of economic extremes, my year of food stamps and of billionaires.

A doorman in a matching burgundy cap, jacket, and pants with gold piping, and white gloves, flung open the door for my boss, Sara, and me and then ushered us through the marble, rococo-inspired lobby, with gold leaf fleurs-de-lis on the walls. "We're here to see Marcy," my boss told him as he escorted us to the elevator, where he pressed the button marked "18." No last name needed; the doormen in our donors' buildings knew every one of their residents and exactly which multimillion-dollar apartment they inhabited. I was a development associate, the second on a team of two tasked with raising money for the small nonprofit that AmeriCorps had assigned me to. When I filled out my AmeriCorps application online, there was a drop-down menu of fields to choose from, and I'd picked "fund-raising" because my dad was a fund-raiser and I knew it involved things I thought I knew how to do, namely, writing and talking to people.

A woman in wash-and-wear slacks and a beige top, which, in my nonexistent experience with domestic help, I would've called an art smock, opened the door to Marcy's apartment and led us down a hallway with an inlaid wood floor. Sitting on a marble-topped mahogany table with carved ballerina legs was a bouquet of white roses and pale pink peonies that was more of a centerpiece than a bouquet, and I wondered briefly if it was left over from someone's wedding. No, I quickly realized, it was just the foyer bouquet, which coordinated with a smaller but no less opulent arrangement on top of the grand piano in the living room where Marcy stood poised for our arrival. She glided across an expanse of white carpeting to embrace Sara and kiss her on both cheeks. I was trying to figure out who the nameless woman in the smock was and found my answer when she silently carried in a tray of tea sandwiches. I then understood that we wouldn't be introduced.

Everything in Marcy's home was precise and immaculate and, by contrast, I felt elephantine. I stood frozen in place on the pristine white carpeting as I inclined my head toward Marcy so that she could kiss my cheeks too. I hadn't washed my hair that morning and flushed with shame that she would smell my lower-class lack of hygiene. I knew Marcy and her lot didn't wash their own hair; they popped over to a dry bar for a blowout. I thought I saw her smooth, pearlescent forehead wrinkle as she rounded my face for the destination of my second cheek, her Chanel earring scratching my skin ever so slightly, leaving an indentation of you-can't-afford-this in its wake. My scalp suddenly felt greasier than the cheap cheese pizza my roommates and I scarfed on the floor of our dining-room-table-less living room. I swear dandruff started to plume.

The kissing ritual over—a bizarre New York City thing

that I never fully understood or felt comfortable with—I turned my head to the left, pretending to look out the floor-to-ceiling window with a view of Manhattan, in order to surreptitiously check if there was any dandruff on the shoulder of what I now realized was a provincial, criminally unfashionable beige suit with thin blue stripes and pleats all the way around the hem of its knee-length skirt. Marcy and Sara were chatting about chemical-peel facials, a conversation I had nothing to contribute to, so I began to inch around the room, taking in the incongruous collection of art on the walls. As far as I could tell, the only unifying thread was that it was all real art by real artists.

Our goal today was to secure a donation from Marcy—perhaps one of these paintings—for our nonprofit's annual gala fund-raising auction at Christie's. Sara also planned to ask her to consider purchasing a dinner table at the event for $25,000. This being a sum nearly three times my annual salary, I couldn't imagine she'd say yes. Even though I knew that to Marcy $25,000 was about the equivalent of $5 to me, I still couldn't comprehend how a person could have enough excess cash to simply give away that much money. In this way, fund-raising felt miraculous to me. I liked that we gave people a chance to help others, a chance to do something meaningful with their money. But I still couldn't fathom the dollar amounts, and was relieved that Sara made the actual ask.

Marcy and Sara were helping themselves to the spread

that the maid had brought in but I hesitated, mortified I'd drop food on something priceless. I wondered if there was any way I could avoid eating without seeming weird. I couldn't feign vegetarianism or an allergy to gluten, since my boss had witnessed me wolf down a cheeseburger when we'd gone out for a team-building lunch the week before. Plus, I was starving and not in a financial or hunger position to turn down a free lunch. So I held my breath while balancing a Limoges plate of ham sandwich on my lap, perched on the edge of a pale rose–colored damask sofa that probably cost more than my undergraduate degree. My legs and back were cramping because I had my knees jammed together and my lower back arched to keep the plate stationary while alternately smiling, saying a few conversationally appropriate words to prove I wasn't mute/an idiot, and taking infinitesimal bites. I looked down and saw a determined run in my nylons making its way from somewhere deep inside my brown, half-inch pumps up the outside of my calf. Every time I shifted it bolted upward. My mom had taught me that if I ever accidentally broke something at another person's house, I should pay to replace it. But there was no way I could afford to even *offer* to replace anything in Marcy's apartment, which made me feel unwelcome in my own mind. I'd only ever been in the homes of people relatively close to my own position on the economic spectrum: people who owned things from Bed Bath & Beyond or World Market and perhaps, on the high end, Pottery Barn, but probably purchased with a coupon or on clearance.

I prayed that we'd move over to the security of the massive dining room table I could see lurking in the next room, replete with its own coordinating floral centerpiece. A plate is so much more stable on a table, so less likely to be dropped onto white carpeting. No luck; we were quite clearly staying in the living room on these unforgiving light-colored surfaces with nowhere to rest cutlery or one's glass of lime-infused sparkling water. It occurred to me that no one who cleans their own home would have this much white/nearly white furniture. Sara, a consummate pro, mercifully did all the talking because I wasn't sure what to say to a person who had hundreds of dollars in floral arrangements delivered to her home every few days. Marcy offered to donate a week at their vacation home in Nice, France, and to purchase a dinner table. Our work was done.

That night, I was drained from maintaining a faux smile and a tenuous perch on Marcy's living room furniture all afternoon. Riding home on the train, I didn't have the energy to read the Brooklyn Public Library book I'd dragged around with me all day. I just sat there and stared at people as they got on and off the subway car. Forty-five minutes later, I was back home in Crown Heights, Brooklyn. There were police cars stationed at every other cross street of Franklin Avenue, and a police observation tower sitting outside of the Yaffa Money Mart bodega three blocks up from my apartment. I walked over to a police car and asked what was going on. The officer told me they were on routine surveillance for drug- and gang-related activity. I asked if I should do anything to protect myself and he said, "Move to a safer neighborhood."

Stunned, I walked home and locked the door. I'd seen a gun not attached to a law enforcement officer for the first time and the inside of a billionaire's home for the first time during my first month in New York City, and the whiplash was almost unbearable. I was starting to feel like I'd made a mistake in coming here, but I couldn't back out now. I was on contract with AmeriCorps for a year and, more to the point, I well knew that nowhere else would hire me without this year of experience on my résumé. So I sat in my windowless bedroom, staring at my cardboard dresser, eating black beans from a can, drinking wine from a box, and wondering how I'd survive the next eleven months.

There wasn't a grocery store in my immediate neighborhood, but after a few weeks my roommates and I found a Key Food eleven blocks away, which had cramped aisles of mostly canned and frozen goods with flyspecked fluorescent lights overhead. Despite reading about them, I'd never understood what it felt like to live in a food desert. I had $120 in food stamps every month, which was another benefit of AmeriCorps. Since my rent was $500 a month and I brought home $833.33 every month (and was trying to save as much of that $333.33 as humanly possible), I couldn't afford to spend any more than the food stamp allotment on my meals. After I figured out I could slip laundry detergent and shampoo in with my groceries and pay for them with my food stamp debit card, I spent even less on actual food. I'm a terrible, not to mention unenthusiastic, cook, so I worked out a rotation of canned tuna, peanut butter (usually without bread), black beans, pasta, and frozen dinners that fit my budget of around $4 or less per day. Since my office provided a pizza lunch every Friday, I'd stuff myself and then take home all the leftovers I could squeeze into a gallon-size ziplock bag I'd bring from home and wash out each week. I was dizzy with excitement the hour before the pizza was delivered, steaming hot and delicious with doughy, garlicky knots as an appetizer. I'd learned about poverty in college, and food deserts specifically, but none of that effectively conveyed what it feels like to carry a week's worth of cheap groceries home, the plastic bag handles digging into my wrists, for an eleven-block walk over urine-soaked sidewalks with people asking me to give them my food and me feeling guilty for not giving it to them because I just could not repeat the ordeal. There was a bodega on my street that sometimes had fresh fruit, so I'd buy apples or bananas on my way into work if they weren't too brown and spotted. I couldn't get over the fact that back in the Midwest, we'd considered it an actual chore to hop in our car and drive a few miles to a gigantic, sparkling, air-conditioned grocery store that played Top 40 and sold every kind of vegetable you could ever want (and a lot that no one ever did seem to want).

"Go back to where you came from!" a woman screamed at me as I pushed my four-wheeled metal cart to the laundromat one Saturday morning. I was walking down the sidewalk with my dirty laundry, so I thought it was pretty obvious that I, in fact, lived here. Up until that point, that moment of being yelled at in the street, I'd assumed I was struggling alongside my neighbors. That we were all poor and on food stamps and desperate together. Every week, we sat side by side on the cracked orange plastic chairs in the laundromat that stank of feet and had washers encrusted with grime around the edges. We all dully watched our clothes rotate since it was well known they'd be stolen, still dripping wet, if we left. But that woman's words, and the naked anger behind them, made me realize that I was a fake. I was just trying on the mantle of poverty for a year, making a cutesy budget to mete out my food stamps and picking up loose change underneath swank Manhattan bars I'd duck into pretending I was meeting a friend, but really just hoping someone had dropped a twenty as they ordered their third martini.

I wasn't living in entrenched, generational poverty with no way out, and I had no one to provide for but myself. What a selfish, entitled brat I was. I'd be gone as soon as my contract with AmeriCorps was over and my lease ended. I had no intention of living here in any permanent sense and my neighbors knew it. They hated what I represented: white, educated, wealthy privilege. Forget my billionaire donors; I'd never understood *my own privilege* in such sharp relief. I hated living in Crown Heights. I hated the yelling at all hours, the gunshots, the mice and cockroaches in our apartment, and the inexplicable incident where someone ripped all the sidewalk trees out of their planters one night, but I've never been more grateful to live somewhere. Without that experience, I wouldn't have a frame of reference for how fortunate I am and for how grinding and chronic true poverty becomes. I wouldn't understand how profoundly fortunate it is to live in a neighborhood you're not terrified to walk through alone at night and that has a grocery store and banks and doctor's offices. I didn't make a conscious choice to live in Crown Heights and at the time, all I could think about was leaving, but it was the best thing that could've happened to privileged, sheltered, twenty-two-year-old me.

I didn't belong in either the living rooms of the wealthy or my neighborhood with its en plein air drug trade. I started to despise both. I learned that I didn't want to be rich after listening to our donors complain about managing their household staffs and which apartment building they could afford to upgrade to and where they'd summer and which elite schools their children would attend. It struck me that most of these people weren't happy in a deep or genuine way. There was too much peer pressure to conform, aspire, strive, and prove their wealth to simply enjoy life.

Moreover, I got the sense that if you're tremendously wealthy, you never know if people are interested in you or in your money. I also saw that some people in this echelon came to define themselves by their wealth more than by any other aspect of their lives. Exactly like my Crown Heights neighbors, some of whom were ruled by their lack of money, the affluent are sometimes ruled by its presence. I didn't want any of that. I felt as though there had to be more to life than an endless acquisition of money in order to continually buy more stuff.

On the other pole of things, I didn't want to be poor, with the attendant desperation, anger, and depression. Both worlds were completely obsessed with money for opposite reasons. I realized that I wanted a life where money wasn't important; and so, in addition to my resolve not to take on debt that year, I decided to save as much as I possibly could. I had no idea if this type of life was even possible, and I knew next to nothing about managing my finances (pitiful as they were) but I figured that the place to start was with money in the bank. And so I began to save.

The upside here was that my plan vis-à-vis Nate seemed to be working. His job in Kansas was a contract position that ended in November, so he decided to look for his next employer on the East Coast. In December, he flew to New York and spent the month holed up in my windowless bedroom, job hunting on the spotty Wi-Fi we "borrowed" from our downstairs neighbors. But what he was more successful at, and has always had an uncanny knack for, is networking. This is how we found ourselves one Thursday night at a bar in Hell's Kitchen that served free hot dogs and how, in true Nate fashion, he left with an interview scheduled at a firm in Boston that married his two great loves (other than me): politics and software engineering. He was hired the next week. In early January, we took the $15 Fung Wah bus up to Cambridge, Massachusetts, to find him an apartment. He settled on a subterranean basement unit with the pros of being in a desirable urban neighborhood and a five-minute walk from his new office. We celebrated with dinner at a BYOB Indian restaurant in the East Village that, for unknown reasons, is covered with Christmas lights. It's also cheap beyond belief, two things I have to believe are correlated. Nate was gone the next week.

Cambridge is a lot closer to Brooklyn than Kansas, but it's still a 217-mile distance in one of the most expensive corridors of the United States. Neither of us owned a car, so we were left with the bus. Let's iron something out right now: a city bus is fine. A city bus is cheerful with a jovial driver and passengers who have recently bathed, all zipping around town with ease. But a long-distance bus? That is an entirely different animal. A long-distance bus is no one's first choice. It's no one's second choice. It's the choice of last resort for people who cannot afford to cross state lines in any other way. *Any* other way, I tell you.

Every Friday at exactly 5 p.m., I'd run from my midtown

office to Grand Central Terminal banging my suitcase (a beaten-up, green, '80s-era hand-me-down from Nate's dad) behind me and ride to the Lower East Side where the Fung Wah bus picked up, standing the whole way so that I could be the first person to bolt off the train and up the station steps. There wasn't a stop or a station per se for the Fung Wah, just a window counter jutting out of a Chinese restaurant where I bought my $15 ticket. Then, no matter the weather, I stood on the sidewalk in a glum queue of people who simultaneously wanted to get to Boston, but did not want to get on this bus, with its inoperable windows and ingrained stench of fish and fried food. I'd slump into an aisle seat and try to look like I had typhoid/anger management issues, hoping no one would want to sit next to me. And no one wanted to sit next to me because we all tacitly agreed that the only thing worse than riding on a bus for four hours is sitting next to a stranger on a bus for four hours, which is what usually happened. A latecomer would rush on the bus, sweating from their jog, victorious they'd made it, and squeeze in next to me, our coats and bags jumbling at our feet and falling down on top of us from the too-small overhead bin. We'd nod apologetically at each other, both knowing we'd prefer to sit alone, but also acquiescing to our new reality. My fellow passengers and I would eat the dinners we'd brought, not making eye contact, facing forward, futilely praying we wouldn't be delayed in the inevitable, inexorable Friday evening rush hour traffic for more than an hour or two. Once, we were stuck for seven hours on the highway in the middle of a blizzard. I've tried to think of worse experiences in my life. The only one that comes even *remotely* close is the time Nate and I flew to Belgium for vacation and I contracted food poisoning in the airport and spent the entire flight running back and forth to the lavatory. The Fung Wah bus service was shut down in 2013 for safety violations, but this was 2007 and they were, somehow, hurtling passengers down the highway, providing a means of transportation for everyone who couldn't afford a $200 train ticket just to get from one state to the next.

At the end of this four-to-seven-hour trudge, Nate would meet me at South Station in downtown Boston and we'd snuggle on the T ride to Central Square in Cambridge. The weekends were how I wanted the rest of my life to be: playing house with Nate. He was it for me; he was my future. We were too poor to do anything, so we'd melt cheese on bread in the toaster oven his parents gave him as a new job present and drink boxed wine by the light of Christmas candles I bought for us in the Walgreens holiday clearance section. We slept late on Saturdays and then walked the length of the city many times over, pausing to read the menus of restaurants we couldn't afford to eat in. The only reason I brought a suitcase every week was to load it up with my dirty laundry, sheets included, and wash it in his in-unit washer/dryer, which was located in the front hall/ living room right behind the couch.

Every Sunday afternoon starting at about 3 p.m., a hollow well of despair bloomed in me. I'd watch the clock, try not to watch the clock, then watch the clock again as my time with Nate ticked down. It was the lowest point of my week, every week. Initially, I took a midafternoon Fung Wah home, but as the months wore on and our ritual of creating a two-person nest deepened, I moved my departure time later and later. I ended up with the 7 p.m. bus, which was the latest I could *possibly* go and still make it to work the next morning by 9 a.m. The Fung Wah dumped me in the fish gut–drenched streets of Chinatown at 11 p.m. Then I'd take two trains back to Crown Heights and walk the eight blocks home guided by whichever streetlights happened to be working that week, trailing my suitcase of clean laundry, nursing my weekly broken heart.

In April, Sara offered me a full-time position to begin after my AmeriCorps tenure ended in September. I was flattered but presented with a dilemma since I didn't want to continue this Fung Wah drudgery. I wanted to move in with Nate, but not without first getting engaged. I thought if I just moved in with him, we might never get married. We'd slide into cohabitation and never see the point of making it official. I'd miss out on that element of adulthood. I was so bent on following what I envisioned as the prescribed steps for achievement that I was convinced marriage had to be part of my life in order for me to be perceived as successful.

Sensing that this was my moment for leverage, I outlined the situation for Nate in one long, awkward sentence that went something like, "My lease is up at the end of August, I want to leave Brooklyn, I'm tired of the long-distance relationship thing, and ideally, I'd move in with you, but I'm not willing to do that unless you're ready to put a ring on it." I figured if he didn't propose soon, he never would.

Eons elapsed (by which I mean a month), no proposal happened, and I started what can only be correctly described as world-class stressing out. What if spending the rest of our lives together wasn't what Nate had in mind? I'd considered our marriage a foregone conclusion since the beginning of our senior year, when I'd returned from eight months of studying abroad and he'd come to the airport *with my parents* (after driving the five hours to St. Louis and *staying at their house overnight without me*). Us not getting married hadn't entered my calculations. I was now twenty-three with very little in savings, and no clear next step other than moving to Boston and getting married. I hadn't made contingency plans because none of my future-casting was without Nate by my side. The job I'd been offered (that is to say, the job I had) would pay $30,000 a year so I'd no longer have access to food stamps or a free MetroCard (another AmeriCorps benefit). By my calculations, that meant I'd still be slogging through white-collar poverty. Both of my roommates had already made plans to move in with other people, and I had no clue where I'd live in New York

City. I certainly didn't want to stay in Crown Heights, but I also had no prospects for roommates. All of my friends were already partnered or roommated up, I couldn't afford to live alone, and I was terrified of moving in with Craigslist strangers.

I was also keenly aware of the financial ramifications of us getting married. Neither of us earned enough at that point to pay rent, buy groceries, and also save anything close to "real" money. The only hope I saw was for us to combine powers. Living together in Nate's tiny one-bedroom would dramatically increase our savings rate and allow us to put some distance between us and a $0 net worth. Yeah, I loved Nate and wanted to spend the rest of my life with him, but I also saw marriage as fiscally prudent. If our salaries were merged in the same bank account, we'd actually be able to shore up a decent emergency fund—a concept I'd recently learned about from my secondhand copy of *Personal Finance for Dummies*. I was also vaguely aware that we were supposed to be saving for retirement, a fairly ludicrous concept when you're a twenty-three-year-old struggling to buy food, but I saw the economizing efficiencies of marriage as a way to get us closer to these desirable, adultlike ends.

A clammy panic wrapped its fingers around my Nate-loving heart. Nate balances out my perfectionist neurosis (example: see above paragraph) and pushes me to be a better, more accomplished person. There's no one I'd rather spend every day of my life with. I even like going grocery shopping with him because he pretends he's a modern art critic when discussing food package labels. No one else does that. If he didn't propose, not only was it going to screw up my whole life trajectory/fact that I'd already made a list of baby names that sound good with Nate's last name, I also had very real logistical concerns come August 31, 2007.

In June, Nate and I took a trip to visit my parents and our college friends who still lived in our college town. On our first day in Lawrence, Kansas, Nate said he wanted to take a walk around campus. We headed out and he took a backpack with him, which I thought was odd because he prides himself on never carrying anything, but he explained it was supposed to rain that afternoon and that he was bringing an umbrella. Nate was speed walking and, at six foot two, he has a way of getting ahead of me, so I was running to keep up. He seemed oddly sweaty so I wondered what was up. Was this a sign that he was on drugs? Sweating, fast walking, a quick pulse, nervous eyes, and an unexplained backpack? I made a mental note to google it later. We came to Budig, the building on campus with the biggest lecture halls, and Nate said he wanted to go inside to use the restroom. *To do drugs?* I wondered. He returned a few minutes later with a janitor who unlocked one of the lecture halls for us. Nate ushered me up the steps and practically pushed me into a chair near the top of the auditorium. The lights were off in half the room so I twisted in my seat to see where a light switch might be.

When I turned around, Nate was down on one knee, my late grandmother's engagement ring in his trembling hands and his mouth moving. He was asking me something that I couldn't understand because I was crying so hard. He looked nervous and asked if these were good tears or bad tears. "Good!" I managed to sputter. He slipped the ring on my finger, the wrong one actually, but that was much more easily remedied than redrafting my entire life plan. I now understood where we were. These were the exact seats we'd sat in the first time we met in a Journalism 101 class the second semester of our freshman year. He told me later he'd read a poem he'd written about our love, but I have no memory of that. All I remember is being filled with over-whelming joy and, if I'm honest, a pretty large amount of relief.

3

The Tumblers of Adulthood

I was twenty-three years old with a hand-me-down diamond ring on my left hand, business cards, and a salary that was real this time, not a mere stipend. I took myself rather seriously at that point and felt like the tumblers of adulthood were clicking into place. Engagement: click; real job: click; living with Nate: click. I was only forward-looking, always pressed into the wind, craning my neck to see what I could achieve next, what more I could cross off of my unending list. I saw the present as my platform for launching into the future, not as something with any merit of its own. There was no resting on laurels or enjoying of the moment for me. Nate and I decided to renew the lease on his basement apartment in Cambridge because it was cheap and conveniently located. We agreed we needed to save money for our future, an amorphous concept, but one which we knew would require more than the combined $8,000 we had in the bank. We wanted to be together and we didn't care that the only sunlight in that apartment snaked through the partially subterranean windows for about an hour every afternoon. It was like trying to line up a Stonehenge equinox to catch an ephemeral ray on your bare forearm.

I'd grown up hearing my parents' stories of their first home, which was a tiny two-story in Denver furnished with hand-me-down furniture from my great uncle's dental practice waiting room. In the summers, it was so hot in their unair-conditioned bedroom that they dragged their mattress down to the cool basement, which had a concrete floor with a drain in the center. Nate's parents scrimped for years to put a down payment on their first home, a nine-hundred-square-foot, brown-carpeted bungalow in Miami with a back porch bigger than the entire first floor. These were the guideposts Nate and I followed. We had no expectation of hardwood floors or new paint or matching silverware. We were both taught that frugality is woven through your early years, that it's integral to how you build a life together. Debt wasn't something either of us ever considered. Living in wealth-saturated Cambridge—home to Harvard, MIT, and a lot of trust funds—Nate and I realized we weren't doing as our peers were doing. They'd upgraded to two-bedroom condos with stainless steel appliances and newly refinished bathrooms. They ordered matching furniture to be delivered from West Elm and Pottery Barn, while Nate and I stuck with the once-white hide-a-bed couch that'd been in the apartment when he moved in. We went to IKEA in a rented car for the rest of our furniture and assembled it ourselves, which at the time I mistakenly thought was the height of frugality.

A month after Nate proposed, and a month before leaving New York City, I was hired as a development associate in the major gifts department at WGBH, which is Boston's NPR and PBS station and the producer of many PBS programs. Since I'd started in development after picking that fund-raising drop-down option for AmeriCorps, I figured the quickest way to advance was to stick with the same field. I knew the terminology, I understood the basics, and I was pretty good at it. Plus, I had the golden résumé goose of "one year of relevant experience." I didn't consider fund-raising my passion, but I didn't actively dislike it either. I was more interested in climbing through the ranks and increasing my salary than I was in doing something I "loved," because I didn't think doing something I loved would bring me any conventional recognition or notoriety. I wanted people to think I was successful and, as far as I could tell, the best way to get there was through a career. More to the point, I wasn't even sure what it was that I loved doing in the first place. I liked to write, but that didn't sound like much of a career to me. I thought getting a solid job was the consummate achievement, and development associate was a step up from AmeriCorps development associate. It didn't occur to me that there was any other path to follow.

Sitting in my assigned cubicle at WGBH, all I could see

was gray. The patterned fabric of the cubicle enclosure was gray, the weapons-grade edges of my metal filing cabinet were gray, my plastic desktop was gray, and the wall behind it, also gray. Staring at the unforgiving rectangle of my computer screen, I was trying to think of a synonym for "generous" while writing a thank-you letter to a donor. I'd opened with "thank you for your generous support" and I couldn't very well end it with those exact same words. I could hear my cubicle neighbor clacking away on her keyboard. She sounded so competent, so decisive with each keystroke, and I imagined her flying through her daily tasks while I pondered the meaning of the word "generous." I wondered if I was the only one who labored over each sentence, considering it an opus, a monument to the career I wanted to build. I settled on "meaningful philanthropy" and pressed "print." My entire year in New York felt like one long, held breath. This was it; I'd finally arrived into adulthood.

Most Mondays through Fridays I sat in my grayscale cubicle on the sixth floor, banging out thank-you letters, proposals, and reports on how our donors' donations impacted the organization. But the summer after I started, I was tasked with planning the logistics for a fund-raising event at a donor's second home on Martha's Vineyard. I'd never been to the Vineyard before, but by this point I'd been inside a number of unbelievably wealthy people's houses, mostly on Beacon Hill. Parachuting into the upper class is part of a fund-raiser's job. Although I wasn't senior enough to actually *ask* these people for a donation, my boss, Ellen, whom I worshipped, sometimes took me with her as a sort of note taker/posse member. I'm articulate, I don't take up much space, and I have very neat handwriting and an ability to capture details from a conversation, all valued qualities in my profession.

I put together an invitation list, which entailed typing out the handwritten names the donor faxed to me, pulling lists from our database, and then mailing out the invitations. RSVPs trickled in and I dutifully recorded whether Mr. and Mrs. VanDam would arrive together or separately, and then made name tags for everyone with a WGBH logo at the top that took me the better part of three hours to line up correctly. Minutiae was the business of my days. Correctly spelling, and knowing, that Professor Rochelle M. Daughtry prefers to go by "Buffy" and that her investment banker husband, in all seriousness, goes by "Bick" was the currency of my role. I arranged for a caterer, unsure what canapés were until I googled them, and hoped that an open bar with only beer and wine didn't reek of a middle-class suburban wedding reception (that being my experience with open bars up to that point).

Usually Ellen was the one to actually attend these events along with her boss, Win, the vice president of development, but Ellen couldn't go and decided to send me in her stead. I did not see this as a good thing. There are so many elements to an event, all of which can go wrong, and all of which the event planner is blamed for. There's a myth that being an event planner is fun because you get to attend an event. But I find that being an event planner is horrifically stressful because you have to attend an event. All of the guests are munching those canapés and throwing back that free beer and wine while you're stress-sweating through your inconspicuous dress, praying that the sound system doesn't crackle when the opening remarks begin, feigning polite conversation, and wondering why on this green earth you didn't wear flats as you shift your weight from the front of your high heels to the back trying to decompress your toes during your fourth hour straight of standing on a concrete floor (every floor feels like concrete after standing on it for four hours straight in high heels). Despite my feelings on all that, I couldn't very well say I wouldn't go. So I tried to convince myself it was a chance to impress my boss's boss—the doyenne of fund-raising, beautiful, stylish, and immaculate in speech and written word—Win.

Three weeks to the event and I already had sweaty palms and nightmares of me toppling a pyramid of wineglasses at a crucial fund-raising juncture. It was decided Win and I would arrive separately, so I left my apartment at 6 a.m. on the morning of the event to allow enough time to walk to the T station, take the train downtown, transfer to another train, walk a few more blocks, ride a bus to the ferry station, take the ferry over the ocean to the Vineyard, and then take a cab to the donor's (second) home on "the island" (as it's known by those in the know, which was most certainly not me).

I quite like traveling alone so while bumping across the ocean on the ferry, with the August sun on my face and salty spray hitting my powdered nose, I forgot where I was going and relaxed into it, smiling for a moment before self-induced pre-event panic weighed down the corners of my mouth into the grim line that constituted my event face. I turned away from the ferry railing and walked inside the boat to sit on a low bench where I could obsessively check the spelling on the name tags in my bag—not that there was anything I could do about an error at this point, being, as I was, on the open ocean.

When the cabdriver pulled up to the address I'd given him, I was certain he'd gotten it wrong. Similar to my arrival at my graffiti-laden Brooklyn walk-up, the property in front of me did not meet expectations. Our donors had described this—their summer home—as "a little Vineyard cottage." In no way were "cottage" or "little" the terms I'd use. As I climbed out of the cab in my sundress and sneakers, which I'd worn on account of the many blocks I had to walk during my three-hour trek to get there, I stood back to take in the estate soaring before me. I walked up to the carved wooden front door, reminiscent of a Frank Lloyd

Wright masterpiece, and hoped I was in the right place since there was no way I could hail a cab on this secluded street, and I didn't have cell reception.

Feeling like a disheveled, overaged Girl Scout, I knocked. The donors could not have been more gracious as they gave me a tour of the grounds and fed me lunch. Mercifully the caterer showed up on time. I dragged a not-too-priceless-looking table in the massive foyer (larger than my apartment) into service as my name-tag command center. There were several hours to go until the event. Having already set up the chairs, arrayed the handouts, and organized the name tags alphabetically, I awkwardly loitered in the donors' cavernous kitchen, where they'd told me to "eat anything you like." I furtively took a bottle of water and an apple because they were the closest items to me and the only things that wouldn't involve me digging through their $20,000 refrigerator; which, by the way, I couldn't find for ten minutes on account of the fact that the exterior was handcrafted wood to match the rest of the cabinetry. I had no idea people had handcrafted refrigerator exteriors. I put the empty bottle of water and the apple core into my backpack because I couldn't find a trash can, figuring it was probably custom-built into a wall somewhere.

Win arrived as scheduled, an hour before kickoff, and I took that opportunity to slip into the guest bathroom and change my clothes. I'd brought my "event outfit" with me, a sleeveless, knee-length, black Ann Taylor dress with a pleat at the back and a demure neckline, which I wore to every single one of these dreadful things. I put on a strand of faux pearls. I think of this as the uniform of fund-raising professionals because it's classic enough that it could be something really expensive, but plain enough that it doesn't stand out, so you're unlikely to upstage or offend any donors, and it works in all four seasons. It's the vanilla ice cream cone of fund-raising events. Or so I'd thought. I was now melting, in both a physical and an emotional sense, from the following combination of issues: it was August on the Vineyard; I was alone at an event with my boss's boss; and I was the one who'd selected the food, made the handouts, gone with only beer and wine, and spelled all the names on the name tags. After mopping off my sweaty self with toilet paper and applying as much deodorant and makeup as I deemed logistically possible, I slipped out and stationed myself behind my name-tag table.

A stream of pastel linen began to arrive. The foyer was starting to resemble a Ralph Lauren ad campaign of fit grandparents with yellow sweaters tied around pink-polo-shirted necks alongside a floral Lilly Pulitzer magazine spread with a few stragglers who'd very clearly walked straight off of a golf course. Not a speck of black fabric among them. I stood like an out-of-place beacon behind my table, the youngest person in the room by a good thirty years and the only one in a formal dress and heels, with my hair pulled into an unfortunate, severe bun on account of an inability to cope with frizziness. Ridiculous as I felt, I knew what I was doing. I'd memorized as many faces as possible ahead of time (thank you, google) so that I could greet guests by name, by preferred nickname at that, and hand them their tags while gesturing toward the cater waiter holding a platter of something vaguely shrimplike to my right. I wondered if I could hide behind the name-tag table for the entirety of the event because I dreaded walking into the cluster of billionaires stationed in the circular living room underneath the timber-framed skylight rotunda.

Win jabbed a glass of white wine into my hand and I wondered what I was supposed to do with it. Pretend to drink it? Pour it into a plant? Hold it aloft and try to exude casual wealth? I decided to mete out tiny sips over the two hours of the event in the hopes that this was what a person was supposed to do with a glass of white wine on the Vineyard. I exhaled with relief when the caterer had a question for me. I hurried into the kitchen with her, hoping Win thought I looked industrious and capable, and that I might somehow be able to stay in there for the next hour or so.

As the event drew to a close, and nothing cataclysmic transpired, I wondered why I'd endured so much anxiety over what amounted to a cocktail party with a few remarks. For the first time ever, I questioned what the purpose of my job was. To facilitate social events among really rich people who mostly already knew one another, in the hopes that they might one day write us a check? I was relieved it'd gone smoothly, but I wasn't sure I felt any sense of personal accomplishment. It was more that I'd done what my boss had asked me to do. I'd executed a straightforward list of tasks. Pressing my back against the donor's designer wallpaper (who knew that was a thing) just to the right of a Picasso, clutching my empty wineglass now fused to my palm via sweat, I felt a sense of vertigo. I envisioned decades of me doing these events, of gradually inching toward the age of most of our donors, of eventually progressing to Ellen's level, and then to Win's, and I wondered what the point was. Would I ever feel like I was *doing* something meaningful and not just incurring ever-higher levels of anxiety? It's not like I'd changed anyone's life or created something lasting or profound. I spent most of my waking hours at my job and after this harrowing fifteen-hour day, which ultimately resulted in nothing concrete I could point to as an achievement, I started to question why.

I was proud of the work NPR and PBS did, and I believed deeply in the mission of WGBH, of bringing unbiased news and information to people. But I was having a hard time seeing my own contributions to that whole. I was a small cog in a mammoth corporate machine and I didn't feel like my work had an impact that meant anything to the overarching end result. My thank-you letters and my name tags seemed like nothing more than stacks of paper people pushed aside as they reached for the more important things of their lives. I didn't suffer self-aggrandizement and

I knew WGBH would keep on going without me. It's not like NPR would go off the air without me occupying my development associate cubicle. I wanted so badly to climb that proverbial ladder, but this event had me questioning why, and if I could slog through another few decades of name tags in order to get promoted to a position that would comprise a crucial element of the system. Would I ever derive personal satisfaction from this type of work? From being a worker bee focused on improving someone else's hive? I'd always pictured myself as part of a team, as someone with a name badge and an identity defined by where I worked, and by what I did. But I was starting to question if that was what I actually wanted to do with my time. I was unfulfilled. I was in turmoil.

Win and I left the donors' home together in a cab and then caught the ferry back to the mainland. Sitting side by side in the plastic chairs that make up the front row of the boat, facing a window overlooking the darkening sky above the ocean, I sensed an opportunity. Win wasn't reading or looking at her phone and we'd already debriefed the event during our cab ride. I decided this could be what I mentally termed a "career advancement conversation," since it was rare I had time alone with the boss of my boss.

Emboldened by that solitary glass of wine on an empty stomach—and while inhaling the almonds I'd packed in my bag since I thought it would be rude to eat canapés during the event—I asked Win something along the lines of, "How do you measure success in your life?" I said the word "life," I remember very clearly, but I assumed she'd discuss how she measured success in her career. Win exudes confidence and professionalism, and I thought of her and Ellen as my ultimate career destination. What I hoped was that we'd steer this around to discussing how *I* could advance and find fulfillment in *my* career.

Win told me she measured her life through her personal successes; through the milestones in her family and their accomplishments. She went on to explain that ultimately, you have to look outside of your job in order to create a well-rounded life. Her reply was the only thing I hadn't imagined her saying. I'd assumed that everything would come from, and through, my job. College had filled that role, as it'd given me a purpose, a social outlet, volunteer work, the opportunity for accolades, a community—it had constituted my entire life. I'd been trying to engineer my job to serve that same function, and now I had confirmation that it wasn't ever going to do that. Between Win's words and my feelings of disappointment after the event, I felt unmoored. This thing I'd held up as my paragon, my ultimate goal—my career—was turning out to be quite a bit less inspiring, exciting, and holistic than I'd imagined.

A few weeks later, as I read over my to-do list one Wednesday morning in my cubicle with Starbucks in hand, I slumped down into my ergonomic office chair, tapping my red patent leather flats against the plastic mat the chair rolled around on. This list could've been from six months ago or even a year. I had a ton to do, but I just kept toggling down my list from top to bottom, and then bottom to top, vainly trying to divine some purpose, some meaning from all this interminable busywork that I was supposed to do. My job had evolved into an exercise in repetition. Sure there was variation, but essentially, I did the same things over and over and over again: assist my bosses in asking for donations, thank donors for making donations, steward those donations, then ask those same donors for another donation, and rev up the gristmill all over again. It was an endless loop of development associate déjà vu. I'd had this job for only a year and a half and I had no idea how I'd do it for the next forty.

Worse still, by the time I got home every night I was exhausted and didn't have the energy to do anything remotely creative or interesting. Most days I went to a yoga class right after work, then Nate and I ate dinner while sitting on our secondhand couch (lacking as we were in a table and chairs), and then it was time for bed. Weekends weren't much better because they mostly constituted a race to prepare for the next week: grocery shopping, errands, cleaning the house, preparing meals for the week, doing the laundry. When was I supposed to figure out what I was passionate about? When would I do something that mattered? Where was the space in my life to uncover deeper meaning? Did a deeper meaning even *exist* for uninteresting, real people like me?

I started walking over to the office cafeteria at 10 a.m. every morning to buy a coffee and again at 3 p.m. for a muffin, just for something to do, something to break up what was becoming my monochromatic workday. Nate and I got married that summer and with the wedding behind us, I felt like I had nothing left to look forward to. I had everything I'd wanted, namely a husband and a career, but I didn't know how I'd maintain this routine and this monotony for the rest of my life.

I was promoted to senior development associate, accompanied by a raise, and decided to start getting my hair cut at a chic salon in Harvard Square that a woman in my office recommended. They massaged my neck, brought me herbal tea, washed my hair, and cut and styled it, for just $120. The fact that I used to eat for an entire month on that same dollar amount didn't register at the time. I worked hard, so I reasoned I deserved to treat myself. What was the point of this job otherwise? I told Nate he should buy the stereo equipment he wanted, we got Thai takeout every Thursday night, and went out to dinner every Saturday. This lifestyle inflation we slowly layered on didn't feel like anything noteworthy at the time. After all, we were still way more frugal than everyone else we knew. We didn't have any debt, we lived in that dungeonlike basement, and we took our lunches to work every day. Nevertheless, our expenses were rising month after month. I'd heard the phrase "lifestyle creep," but I didn't think it applied to Nate and me.

The problem was that spending all this money didn't make me feel any better. It didn't get me any closer to feeling like I had a purpose. I mean it was nice, but I realized that aside from the basic improvements it provided of living in a safe neighborhood (with an in-unit washer/dryer) and an ability to buy healthy groceries, this extra spending wasn't increasing my happiness at all. I thought Nate and I needed to aim higher so we decided to buy a house. Or rather, to save up to one day buy a house. That gave us a goal, a long-term joint project that we could discuss and plan for and work on together. Nate and I are at our best when we're collaborating, and buying a house in one of the most expensive real estate markets in the world was a darn good project.

We started going to open houses every weekend to give our dream some substance. We couldn't afford a single thing on the market in Cambridge, but the knowledge that our money was going toward something tangible made all the difference. I still got my fancy haircut and we still ordered Thai takeout every week, but we thought twice before going out for drinks or shopping at Whole Foods. When we first moved in together, I'd managed to save $2,000 of my $10,000 AmeriCorps stipend and Nate had $6,000 in the bank. Sharing this crystallized goal of a home had a tremendous impact on our financial behavior. In 2008 alone, we saved $29,100 of our combined take-home salary of $69,730, which gave us a savings rate of forty-two percent. For two twenty-four-year-olds, we were doing pretty well. We made a lot of money for our age and we managed to save a lot of money for our age. In retrospect, we could've saved even more, but since we were still unaware of the powers of extreme frugality, this was pretty decent. We were on a mission.

In a weekly staff meeting that fall, I chose a chair on the far side of the conference room so that I could stare out the window overlooking the parking garage, which was a better view than the blank whiteboard on the opposite wall. I always got to meetings early, not because I was keen, but because I wanted to pick my seat. Plus, it was an easy way to brownnose. I was sizing up my colleagues around the table, wondering how they all did it. How they looked so engaged and genuinely interested in what we were discussing. I was pretending to take notes in order to stay awake and, since I have such neat handwriting, I realized anyone could read what I was writing, sitting jammed up next to each other as we were so that everyone could have an equal place at the table and didn't have to hug the wall in a folding chair. I wrote down every other word Win was saying while thinking about where Nate and I should go to dinner that Saturday.

Then I heard Win say the word "layoff." I reared my head up and wondered what we were talking about. Why hadn't I been listening?! She went on to explain that every department was being required by management to lay off a specified, but undisclosed to us, number of people. My body temperature rocketed and my face burned with anxiety. The last time I felt this level of concern in public was when I almost fell off a chair in front of my entire fifth-grade class, boys included, while tacking up my drawing of a leaf to the bulletin board. I was cemented to my swivel chair and clamped my eyes on Win, my pen frozen midword above my notebook. I was afraid to glance around the room, thinking that might implicate me somehow. Don't guilty people avoid eye contact? Or do they make eye contact?!?

Either way, I decided the best course of action was to remain stationary. I whirred through all of my transgressions: being late on occasion, missing edits in letters, forgetting to sign donor files out of the file room; but most of all, most dangerous and damning of all was the clawing, growing apathy I felt about my job. Was it obvious? Did my bosses know my inner thoughts? Had I let them seep out, unfiltered, in word or in deed? When the meeting ended, everyone filed out silently, like you do at a funeral when it seems boorish to make small talk. I looked at my feet and hid in my cubicle for the rest of the afternoon, gossiping covertly with my colleagues, which was hard to do since our cubicles weren't offices.

A week later, Nate's boss made a similar announcement and that night, I stewed in our combination living room/ foyer/laundry room while drinking Trader Joe's imitation prosecco. I shouldn't have been surprised. It was 2008 and all the news ever talked about was the Great Recession. Until now, it'd seemed like a problem for other people in other places with other jobs. I was grateful Nate and I had set our goal of buying a house because it meant we had a bunch of money saved up. Unlike all these investment bankers we kept hearing about who'd lived paycheck to enormous paycheck, Nate and I could afford to lose our jobs but still eat and pay rent. We calculated we could last at least a year without either of us being employed, and probably longer.

But it wasn't the money that I was most worried about. It was the shame. How would I walk out of my office with my framed wedding photos and stash of desk snacks in a cardboard printer paper box and admit to everyone that *I'd* been the one laid off? That *I* was the worst employee? What would I do? No companies were hiring, and it's not like I had decades of illustrious experience to fall back on. I called my parents and asked if we could move in with them if job Armageddon happened and they said of course. I'm a worst-case scenario-ist, but also a pragmatic planner. I needed contingencies.

Every time Ellen called me into her office for the next few weeks, I was certain this was it for me. One afternoon I heard her calling my name and I just didn't move. I could feel sweat in unfortunate places. After a self-indulgent minute of allowing my short career to flash before my eyes, I stood up and, ready to pass out, walked what felt like a perp walk the ten feet to her office.

Turns out, I'd overreacted, as perfectionists are wont to do, and neither Nate nor I got laid off. But it scared us. The idea that our jobs could be pulled out from under us with little warning ushered in a new way of thinking about money. Our parents had raised us with the assumption that jobs are secure, that they provide for you and that if you work hard, you'll always be fine. It didn't feel like that was the reality anymore. And it wasn't. We started to save even more of our take-home pay every month. Just in case.

Back in college, my life changed every semester and I'd thrived on that diversity. Now, I'd been in the same job for three years, we'd been living in the same basement apartment for three years, and I wanted something different. In my infinite wisdom, I decided the solution was to go to graduate school. Since college had been such a complete, wholly satisfying experience for me, I wanted to re-create it, to regress into the comfort of student life. I also saw a master's degree as a hedge against potential future layoff scenarios since I'd be more senior, with a richer résumé and an MA after my name. I goaded myself on with the promise that it was another thing to achieve, another gold star. Another external accolade I could stash away in my arsenal of empty successes that I assumed would somehow, someday transmute into happiness.

Nate and I liked Cambridge, a lot more than Brooklyn or Kansas, but we craved adventure. We'd been traveling abroad for vacations every year over the Thanksgiving week (because international flights are cheap then), but that wasn't enough. We wanted to test out living in a new city. Washington, DC, seemed like the best candidate. It had universities where I could go to grad school; it was urban, which was what we were now accustomed to; and Nate's organization was interested in sending him there to be their Capitol Hill presence. I did some research and learned I could go to grad school for free if I worked full time at a university. Since I had zero intention of going into debt for the first time ever, that sounded perfect. I was getting in the habit of up and moving any time I wanted a change, but it didn't bother me because I was young and wanted to experiment with living in different places, with different iterations of myself. Nate and I were twenty-six, unencumbered, and unsure of how we wanted to spend the rest of our lives. It was time for us to move on.

4

A Different Kind of Grindstone

On a warm, breezy Saturday, May 15, 2010, Nate and I moved into a rented, historical, furnished townhouse in the tree-lined Capitol Hill neighborhood of Washington, DC. We'd thrown off the confinement of our basement apartment and taken on a fairly pricey two-story house for no better reason than because we thought we deserved it. Our buying-a-house goal, while still present, had receded in deference to this new trajectory we'd put ourselves on. I'd secured what I'd set out to secure: I worked full time as a fund-raiser for American University and then walked across campus to my masters of public administration graduate classes almost every night, which sometimes lasted until 11 p.m. I was hustling. I was a hard worker. I was miserable.

There were bright orange flecks of powder stuck to the corners of each page in my Management Theory textbook. I'd read a section, take a few notes, highlight a sentence, then eat another Cheeto. After scraping the final dregs of imitation cheese and crumble from the recesses of the bag,

I moved on to the Doritos sitting underneath the desk in our guest bedroom. When I wasn't taking a weekend class, I was holed up in this room studying, with bags of junk food I'd walk to 7-Eleven to buy on Friday nights because I was too embarrassed to put them on our regular grocery list. I didn't want Nate to know how much of this stuff I was eating.

I can't say that I cared what I was learning in grad school; I just wanted to put MA on my résumé because I felt inadequate without it. No one told me to do this. Neither of my bosses at WGBH said I'd earn more if I got a master's, and there's no direct correlation to advancing in the field of fund-raising. But when I panned my office in Boston, I saw that almost everyone above me had an MA of some sort, ranging from Spanish language to vocal performance to business. And my dad, who had a successful career as a fund-raiser for colleges and universities, has a PhD. I felt like a pseudointellectual without a master's degree. Cambridge, home to Harvard and MIT (not to mention the 9,109,034 other universities in the Boston area), has one of the highest concentrations of people with advanced degrees in the country. Living there, I was embarrassed by my provincial BA from a university that no one in the Northeast had ever heard of before, unless they were college basketball fans. I wanted to prove myself academically and decided that excelling at my job alone wouldn't be enough for what I envisioned: a rapidly ascending career commanding respect, a high salary, and good clothes. Never mind my disenchantment with this career; I still saw it as the only way to the top. What I was going to do once I got to this vague "top" remained a mystery to me.

Halfway through my degree program, I'd physically and mentally exhausted myself and, while compulsively eating grapes in order to stay awake during an 8 p.m. to 11 p.m. nonprofit management class one Thursday night, I realized I'd done the wrong thing. I'd wanted to do what other people thought was impossible, work full time while going to school full time, and now that I was in the exact middle of it, I felt like I couldn't back out. I could not abide the sunk costs. I'd gotten this job expressly for the purpose of earning free tuition. Nate and I had moved to DC expressly for the purpose of me going to this school. I didn't see any option except to slog through to the end. I hate being wrong, so when Nate suggested I bail on grad school, I screamed that he didn't understand me. The more he tried to pry me away, the deeper I sunk my fangs into my choice, like a defensive, stubborn leech.

Our townhouse was almost an hour away from campus, so it was easier for me to spend more and more time there and, as a consequence, away from Nate. He, and everything else I used to enjoy, like yoga, taking walks, and sleeping a normal number of hours every night, felt like a distraction from my goal of getting straight As while holding down my job. I had to start painting my fingernails every Sunday night so that I wouldn't frantically rip them off as I studied on the train into work every morning. The only time I saw Nate was to argue over who should order the groceries that week. Giving up on actually going to the store, we now paid Stop & Shop to bring them up our front steps. Finally, Nate started making the order without asking me to avoid the fight altogether.

My mom and dad came to visit us for Christmas that year because we had an actual guest room for them to sleep in. I was so proud to host them in our home and not in a belowground one-bedroom that had forced them to stay in a hotel. I was thrilled to show them this metric of maturity: "Look! A guest room!" While they were in town, I asked my mom to go to Kohl's with me because I needed bigger clothes, which I didn't want to admit to anyone, but was also too depressed to buy alone. Since my mom is the person who took me on the most embarrassing shopping trip of my entire life—to buy my first bra—I felt like she was the only one I could trust. I knew I was gaining weight, but I rationalized it along with everything else: it had to wait until after I graduated. The more grad school stressed me out and crunched my time, the more money we spent. Nate and I were growing less reliant on each other, and more reliant on money to solve our problems. And the more we paid for, the less we communicated and collaborated. Going out to dinner together on Saturday nights became one of the only meals we shared. There wasn't time for the two of us, between my school schedule and the rota of cocktail parties Nate was expected to attend for his job. I kept telling myself that everything would be different when I graduated. Everything would be fine then.

A year into this inhuman schedule, Nate asked me to go hiking with him one Saturday morning. I rolled my eyes and retorted something along the lines of, "Sure I'd *love* to go hiking while studying for my econ quiz and writing a paper on public administration policy." He didn't reply and just looked down at his hands, spread out on the dining room table in front of him, enclosing his coffee mug in the triangle created by his thumbs and forefingers. He was hurt. A gulf had grown between us the whole time we'd been in DC. It was a toxic place for us. Aside from my own terrible work/school decision, DC as a culture operates on how powerful you can make yourself seem. We found it to be a conformist pressure cooker with few extracurriculars beyond self-promotion. Living there and working in the food processor of politics was grinding Nate down. He couldn't even take refuge in the cocoon of our marriage anymore because I was never around. Beyond grad school being the wrong choice, DC was the wrong choice for us. Before moving there, I'd thought we were a hard-charging power couple destined to climb our respective corporate ladders. We would be driven by our American exceptionalism. But after actually *living* that way, I realized we were laid-back midwesterners who appreciate authenticity and solitude, two things DC lacks in gross proportions. We didn't belong there. So I capitulated and agreed to go hiking, even though tromping around in some tick-infested woods sounded like about the worst use of my time imaginable. I'd probably get Lyme disease, which I hoped Nate would feel really guilty about.

I had to wear one of Nate's exercise shirts on account of the weight I'd gained. I passive-aggressively studied in the front seat as Nate drove to a trailhead in Rock Creek Park, the forest incongruously smack in the middle of urban DC. As soon as we got out of the car, I started an inner monologue centered around the theme of what a gigantic waste of time this hike represented. *I needed to study and if not study, do some laundry, which was bursting out of the small hamper sitting next to my dresser in our bedroom. Wait, maybe I should just buy a larger hamper? How long can dirty laundry sit before mold grows? Could I skip part of the reading for my theory class on Monday or would that mess up my participation grade? Maybe I could make some general commentary to make it sound like I'd done the reading. I wonder if my boss thinks I should've asked that donor for a bigger gift? I cannot believe I am walking around these woods when I have an econ quiz on Tuesday. This hike was not on my eighteen-point list for today and I have no idea how I'm going to cram it all in before work on Monday. And lunches! I have to make my lunches for this week. And paint my nails.*

I nurtured this withering, silent diatribe for at least the

first forty minutes of the hike. But after a while, I started to forget about myself. I started to allow the hike to overtake me in the all-encompassing way that only the natural world can manage. Nature is resolute in its age, its splendor, and its absence of concern over my trifling little life. If you ever want to know the true size of things, go walk in the woods for a few hours. I lifted my head instead of staring down at my feet, which were stumbling over roots and rocks. I looked up into the canopy of spring where green leaves and blossoms were suspended overhead. I began to think about my breathing, the rhythmic inhalations and exhalations timed with my feet stepping one in front of the other. I was exhausted, stressed, and out of shape. But I could set that aside right now and think only about walking through this forest. I looked out into the dense poles of hardwoods and softwoods. It was silent except for creatures—squirrels, chipmunks, birds—scuttling through the undergrowth. Nate and I crossed streams. We couldn't hear traffic, we couldn't see buildings, we scarcely saw another person. Rock Creek Park is a perfect beginner's hike; we were basically on a flat trail through some woods the entire time. I was mesmerized by the beauty and simplicity of trees growing out of soil and then staying put in that one spot: observant, omniscient, and without judgment.

After an hour and a half on the trail, I began crying with relief. I hadn't known how badly I needed this reprieve from my stress. My legs ached; I was sweating, breathing hard; and I could feel a blister forming on my left little toe, but I was overcome with a sense of calm. I was wholly focused on my body's mechanics and the silence of the woods surrounding me. I felt an absence of pressure for perhaps the first time in my life, certainly for the first time since moving to DC. I wanted nothing while I was on the trail. I didn't need to impress anyone. I didn't need to do anything but walk. When we looped back to our car, I was already filling with the fevered enthusiasm of a convert, so we set off on another circuit. By the time we drove home that evening, watching dusk settle over man-made monuments to power, which seemed pointless and profligate in a world that contains hundred-year-old trees, all I had to say was, "Can we do this every weekend?" I don't think it's an overstatement to call hiking my salvation.

Nate and I texted each other all week long about where we wanted to hike on Saturday. It was the first time in years that we'd shared the intimacy and urgency of a common goal. We kept our word and went to Great Falls Park in Virginia that Saturday, and to Sky Meadows the Saturday after that. We discovered the Shenandoah National Forest, which is just a few hours from DC, and started making our way through its trail system. After mastering the flat hikes, we began climbing mountains.

We transformed into other people on the weekends. We escaped the tension and anxiety of DC politics, of work, of school. We were simply Nate and Liz, reliant on our bodies and each other to scale mountains. After two months of hiking every weekend, we decided we were ready for Old Rag, an infamously challenging nine-mile loop of rock scrambles with 2,415 feet of elevation gain. We weren't sure we were physically ready, but we wanted to do it, so we did. Sitting at the summit, eating our peanut butter sandwiches, we finally talked about something other than who would order the groceries. Hiking didn't have any of the things I'd spent my young life chasing—success, accomplishment, notoriety—and it was liberating.

Nate and I developed rituals around hiking. We started going to bed early on Friday nights, so that we could get up at 4 a.m. in order to reach distant trailheads in time to summit and descend before nightfall. I loved those early mornings of driving through the still-sleeping city, sipping the thermos of coffee Nate had packed for me, my shoes off, my legs folded underneath me in the passenger seat. I always felt like we were getting away with something, like we'd stolen time. We never went hiking with anyone else because it became our private, sacred time. It was the time when we weren't beholden to other people's schedules or demands or requirements. It didn't matter how long it took us to climb a mountain; we weren't competing against anyone. When we were on the trail, time was immaterial. The only thing that existed in our universe was the two of us and the woods. We'd occasionally pass other hikers, usually also silent, reverent, and engrossed in the spirituality of our pursuit. Nate and I rarely spoke during our ascents.

Climbing a mountain isn't easy and the physicality pushes out unnecessary, clogging thoughts. In the most literal sense possible, it clears the mind. There is no space for anything other than where you can get a foothold in a rock ledge and which tree branch you can grab on to for balance. Cresting the final few miles to a summit is a transcendental experience. On peaks that are high enough, trees don't grow after a certain elevation. You cross that tree line and are on bald, rocky mountaintop with scraggly, hardy brush snaking its way out of crevices, somehow surviving as icy winds whip in your face seemingly from every direction. I was my most intensely focused at this stage because my legs were tired and I needed to maintain good balance in order to not slide down the rocky face of the mountain. Sometimes I would drop to all fours, lowering my center of gravity, which made me feel more secure. And then, in what felt simultaneously like hours and mere seconds, you've summited. Standing on the peak of a four-thousand-foot mountain that I've climbed is all the exhilaration and achievement I've ever needed. On every single summit I've ever climbed my life feels small; not insignificantly so, but reassuringly so.

I didn't quit school or my job, but somehow, I made space for our weekly hikes. I came to understand a maxim that guides me to this day: I can make time for whatever I want to do most. Full stop. My grades didn't even slip because I had the mental decompression and energy reset of strenuous exercise. Hiking gave me what I'd always lacked: self-confidence, perspective, and acceptance. It was the first time in my adult life that I prioritized something that didn't have a clear benefit or route to productivity. I felt like everything else I did was in service of the external metrics of a person's success. Hiking was all my own. It was what brought me peace. I know the exact date of our first hike together, May 21, 2011, because as it turns out, that day changed the rest of my life.

5

That One Time We Bought a House

But I have only four months left until I'm done with my master's degree! This thought scrolled on repeat through my overtaxed brain.

I'd taken a risk in forgoing the dress-code nylons. If I'd known I'd find myself here—in the office of the vice president of development (the boss of my boss) at American University—I most *definitely* would've worn the nylons. The backs of my legs were so sweaty that I couldn't shift my weight in the overstuffed brown leather armchair I was now glued to, because it would make that squelch that's indistinguishable from a fart and makes you wonder if you need to say, "Oh that's just the chair," which then makes everyone absolutely certain it's *not* the chair. So I sat perfectly still, ramrod straight, my wedding rings digging into my clenched fingers because I'd accidentally folded my hands the wrong way and couldn't correct the error because the middle finger on my right hand was now bleeding thanks to the corner of my grandmother's art deco diamond, and I didn't want to introduce another bodily fluid into the situation.

The vice president of development had called me in here forty-five minutes ago with no prior warning and zero indication of his intentions. The moment his assistant's extension showed up on the phone in my cubicle, I was certain I was getting fired, this being how the brain of an underconfident perfectionist works. And so here I sat in a growing pool of my own sweat and blood, racking my brain for which infraction they'd gotten me on. The only two reasons I'd kept this job were the tuition remission and the excellent two-to-one matching 403(b) retirement program. I was trying to puzzle out if these were fireable offenses. It crossed my mind to act pregnant since I'd gained all that weight (never mind that thanks to hiking I'd lost most of it), so I sort of puffed out my belly and wondered how pregnant you had to be in order to qualify as a protected class.

Striding around his many-windowed corner office, gesturing in the air, and adjusting his bow tie, the vice president of development was casually asking me what I considered to be an increasingly nosy line of questions for someone about to be fired. "Do you enjoy DC?" "How's your husband's job here?" "How's your degree program going?" I rattled off "Yes," "Fine," and "Fine," trying for the sake of professional women everywhere not to burst into tears. After twenty-five minutes of this one-sided interrogation masquerading as building rapport between colleagues, he sat down behind his expansive desk, smiled, and said, "I'm sure you know why you're here." I then experienced a rare moment of finesse and simply said, "I'm sorry, I don't, actually." It was an act of divine mercy that I mustered such restraint because, as it turned out, he was offering me a job. Not a job that was a mere step above my current role, but a whole other echelon of job: a director-level job. I'd have my own office, several people reporting to me, a salary more than double what I currently made, and required attendance at director-level meetings (at which I'd heard scones were served). I sincerely have no idea what exactly I said in order to extract myself from that conversation, but I managed a noncommittal response and promised to get back to him soon. I was so relieved I wasn't getting fired that I forgot about the bloody finger situation, which was unfortunate since I decided to use my skirt to surreptitiously mop the leg sweat off the chair before standing up. I now had a bloodstained skirt, an offer for a job I didn't want, and another job that I also didn't want but was using expressly for the benefits. In an act of maturity, I called in sick the next day.

The problem with this job offer was that Nate and I had made the decision, while on a hike a few months before, that we were done with the grubby slickness of DC. But not yet. I needed to keep working at AU until August in order to finish my master's degree. I thought it would be poor form to take this promotion knowing I'd be there only another four months. How was I going to decline a raise but not quit?! I was so insecure about my work that it never occurred to me I'd be tapped for such a big promotion. I have no perspective whatsoever when it comes to the quality of the work I do. To say I'm my own worst enemy would be like saying that a fox is a reddish-furred mammal with a bushy tail. I really should've taken a hint here that I was good at what I did, because this wasn't even the only job offer I had at the time. Ellen, my former boss from WGBH, was in the process of creating a new position and had jokingly emailed to say I'd be the perfect candidate except for the fact that I lived in the wrong state. It was kismet that earlier that week Nate and I had agreed we wanted to go back to Cambridge the minute my classes were over.

It didn't occur to me at the time that maybe, *just maybe*, springing from city to city and fund-raising job to fund-raising job with Pollyanna certainty I'd find happiness *this time* was a tad—just a *tad*—like the definition of insanity: repeating the same behavior over and over again and expecting different results.

I was blindered by a compulsion to achieve and the job Ellen offered me was a jump up, with people to manage, and a fine salary. Although no office, which did irk me. Going back to that gray, windowless cubicle wasn't exactly the blaze of glory I had hoped for, but it would do. I turned in my final paper for grad school on Friday, August 10, 2012, and started at WGBH as the manager of donor relations and communications on Monday, August 13. I don't let moss grow, which is also how Nate and I bought our first home in a single weekend.

One of the reasons we wanted to move back to Cambridge was the fact that we knew the real estate market there really well on account of having visited roughly 270 of its open houses over the years. Is that an outrageous number of open houses to visit? Oh most certainly, but we're nerds obsessed with making ourselves quasi-experts in whatever we do. Nate and I have a belief that the only people with our best interests at heart are us. It's not that real estate agents would intentionally steer us wrong, it's just that we wanted our own base of knowledge to rely on. Plus, the more money you spend on a house, the more money your real estate agent makes; thus, your incentives and theirs are not entirely aligned. Back in our basement-dwelling days, going to open houses on the weekends was one of our chief sources of entertainment. It was free, it involved strolling around the city, and best of all, snooping on other people's lives via a method that was much more gratifying than Facebook, but far less illegal than, say, stalking. Real estate became a hobby of ours, perhaps a less conventional hobby than hiking or the Russian language classes we took, but also more instructive (especially considering that neither of us ever progressed beyond "hello," "very good," and "I love to travel"). On Friday nights, Nate would map out a route that'd enable us to hit the maximum number of houses that weekend. Since the same places were often open on both

Saturday and Sunday, he'd scout different itineraries for each day. Realtors started to recognize us.

Going to a multitude of open houses was a way to educate ourselves on what we wanted in a home, what to expect in the Cambridge market (not much and for a lot of money), and how to look at a house for its long-term value, not just the superficial, HGTV-promoted practice of "I really like this backsplash." Buying a house is about facts, not feelings, because—ultimately—a home is an investment. Yes, it's a very large investment and one in which you will live and perhaps raise your children, but all these factors aside, it shouldn't be an entirely emotional decision. Nate and I were interested in price per square foot, whether or not it was in a condo association and, if so, the association's rule on nonowner-occupied units and the dollar amount of their reserve. We grilled real estate agents and took home their glossy, full-color info packets for condos that started at $450,000 and ascended steeply from there. It was immaterial to us that we didn't have enough in the bank to cover even the closing costs (let alone the down payment) because we were gathering data that we'd later mine.

Plus, it was fun. After each open house jaunt, we'd walk over to a coffee shop, usually the Atomic Bean on Massachusetts Avenue because they had a divine hummus and veggie plate, and have an earnest conversation about which of the properties we'd buy (you know, if we actually had the money to buy it). From the intensity of our debates,

I'm sure everyone around us thought we were some really indecisive people who unsuccessfully tried every weekend for five years to buy a house. These exercises honed our combined real estate prowess. Nate and I could walk into a house and know within five minutes whether or not it was a good deal, what the other person would think of it, what the real estate agent had done right/wrong with the staging, and whether or not it would sell for over asking price (nothing in Cambridge ever sold for under).

Since Nate monitored what houses actually sold for, he quickly learned that if an asking price seemed like a steal, it was destined for a rash, fisticuffs bidding war where buyers would forgo contingencies and inspections and might even offer all cash. Desperation was the undercurrent of the white-hot Cambridge market. We watched the spectacle as unrepentant voyeurs. I'd dialed back our open house hobby while in DC (because: school, work, and then hiking), but we'd frequented them often enough to stay fresh. Additionally, Nate found he couldn't give up tracking the Cambridge market from afar, so he studiously maintained his spreadsheets detailing asking and closing prices for single and multifamily homes in desirable neighborhoods.

Thanks to our five years of mono-goal saving, by the time we were financially ready to buy in late spring 2012 we were classically overprepared. Our real estate agent kept asking if we were real estate agents. I think he finally resigned himself to the idea that we were nutso nerd yuppies fixated on finding a good deal. When Nate and I want to do something, we throw ourselves into researching like a dog devouring a partially eaten hamburger you brought home from a restaurant and accidentally left in its takeout box on the floor overnight. Having done that once, I can tell you it's pretty intense.

Although we assumed we wanted to buy in Cambridge proper, in deference to my tendency to overresearch, I decided we should explore the closest-in, least-suburby suburbs. The nearest Boston suburbs are not much cheaper than the city; it's just that you get to add a postage stamp of grass to your annual Christmas card photo on your front porch as opposed to wall-to-wall concrete and attached neighbors. To simulate life as suburbanites, we performed the ultimate real estate test (in my mind, anyway): the sample commute. At 5 p.m. on a Friday evening, we left from the parking lot of my once and future employer (WGBH) and wended our way to Nate's office in Somerville, pretended to pick him up, then joined the 87,972 other cars whose owners had decamped to the suburbs. We bailed an hour into sitting immobilized on Massachusetts Avenue, trying to inch our rental car's nose across the city line to suburban Arlington. The thought of driving another three miles to our prospective house was inconceivable. And there ended the possibility that Nate or I would ever live in the suburbs, because there was no way we were going to lose hours of our lives to commuting in exchange for a backyard and a garage. I mused: *What's the point of buying more house and more yard if we're never there to enjoy it? If all our time is spent driving to and working jobs we probably don't even like in order to pay for a house we never get to go to when the sun's out . . . how is that an improvement?*

Bigger houses are one of the more insidious elements of lifestyle inflation. They lure us into thinking we'll solve our problems and reach bliss if only we spend just a *little* bit more money for a little bit more square footage. And so we stretch our budgets in order to eke out an extra bedroom in a desirable school district. Then, we're so heavily mortgaged that we've ensured we need to keep working that job we don't like for a very, very long time. Our culture indoctrinates the idea that we should continually upgrade ourselves to nicer houses, fancier cars, and all-around better stuff. There are few champions for simple, sustainable living that doesn't involve aggressive commutes and bills we can barely cover and reliance on our employers for each and every dime of our paychecks. Nate and I mulled this over, peaced out, and U-turned the car while our once-potential future selves slogged their way, an inch at a time, one person to a car, zoned out to radio stations that reminded them of when they were seventeen and driving was the ultimate freedom, toward mortgages in the apocryphal promised land of suburbia.

Nate and I found our home the next morning during our specialty: an open house. Our real estate agent offered to set up a private showing, but we do our best work alone; I like the incognito state of an open house. Before I'd even climbed the stairs to the second floor, I knew we'd be putting in an offer primarily based on the fact that this was a single-family home: a proverbial hen's tooth in Cambridge. Most homes in Cambridge are condos, since space and housing stock are limited in light of historical regulations that largely prevent high-rise apartments. Another factor tightening the housing market is Cambridge's booming population, girded by the presence of not only Harvard and MIT, but the burgeoning number of biotech firms now headquartered there. Artisanal pickle shops, doughnut bakeries that sell out by 9 a.m., and more yoga studios than banks add to Cambridge's hipster urban appeal. People want to live there and there aren't many housing units available, so the places that *are* available are typically quite small and quite expensive. In our self-guided real estate education process, Nate and I learned a number of not-so-great things about condo associations: they charge fees and assessments, they can tell you what to do with your property, and their rules can restrict (or prevent) your ability to rent out your unit. *Rent it out?* I imagine you're wondering. *I thought you freaks were just now buying it?* True. However. Nate and I, above all else, crave options. We do not like to be hemmed in, so the ability to rent out a house we'd buy, and generate revenue from it, would grant us some serious flexibility. I'd be lying if I said we knew what we wanted those options to *be* at that point in time, but the desire to build alternatives into such a mammoth purchase was important to us. We subscribe to the theory that you never know what's going to happen, you never know when you might want out of a situation, and liquid cash and assets are what grease opportunity. Money doesn't make you happy, but money provides the freedom to find out what *does* make you happy.

Based on the facts that, at the time, over 65 percent of units in Cambridge were rented and rental prices in the area were high and climbing higher, we'd hatched a plan to someday flip whatever we bought into a rental property. And this house, located in the rapidly gentrifying neighborhood of Inman Square, was ideal because it was a rare exception: a single-family home with two stories and a basement, four bedrooms, two baths, and over 1,600 square feet. It was, by Cambridge standards, a McMansion. It was also ugly, had negative curb appeal, was located behind what had formerly been a crack den (not in a hyperbolic sense), and it showed like something out of a '70s sitcom that never made it past the pilot episode. I'm talking lace doilies on every surface, enough bleeding crucifixes to scare the former Catholic in me, and family photos covering so much wall space I could barely tell what the living room paint color was (probably for the best, as it turned out).

All that aside, this house was walking distance to Harvard, MIT, a T station, numerous bus lines, and a burgeoning corridor of restaurants, coffee shops, and yes, one artisanal pickle shop. Our real estate agent disclosed to us that if we didn't buy it, he was going to. Best of all, this house didn't need a gut renovation because the previous owners had done the yeoman's work of putting in hardwood floors, stainless steel appliances, granite countertops, and knocking the 1880s straight out of the floor plan by opening up the kitchen, living room, and dining room. Even the bathrooms were of this decade. Thanks to its erstwhile crack den neighbor (which had been purchased by a developer and was being transformed into high-end condos) and its abominable interior décor (did I mention there were ferns everywhere?), this house sat on the market for an unheard-of fifty days in a city where most properties are snapped up in their first weekend. The next morning, sitting in the terminal at Boston's Logan Airport waiting to board our flight back to DC, we signed the offer letter on my phone, using our fingers to scrawl elementary-school-worthy signatures. Our years of research were vindicated. We bought the house for the lowest purchase price per square foot that entire buying season in all of Cambridge, which of course we knew because Nate never stopped tracking the market (I'm pretty sure he still does it to this day).

I wrote my final grad school paper using our washing

machine as my desk while Nate and our movers loaded the truck in DC. We drove up in our minivan—eating at Arby's along the way to touch base with our midwestern childhoods, since Arby's doesn't exist in cities—and pulled into Cambridge on a steamy August night. We were twenty-eight years old, in a house we owned, sitting side by side on the twin-size air mattress we were using as a couch, with our backs propped against the living room wall, our bare feet planted on the cool, hardwood floor to keep the mattress from sliding out from underneath us. We'd been living large in our furnished townhouse the past few years, and now we owned our own huge (by our standards) and empty (by anyone's standards) home. We had about six pieces of furniture, one of which was a card table and four others of which were folding chairs.

We decided right there on our air mattress couch that it was time to adopt a dog. In DC, we used to walk five blocks to a dog park and sit on a bench watching the dogs romp. Dogs, being dogs, would rush up and jump in our laps. Dog owners, assuming we were one of them, would smile knowingly and ask us our dog's name, at which point we had to awkwardly explain that although we were *in* a dog park, we didn't actually *own* a dog. We were merely doing firsthand research. Much like our open-house sojourns, every time we saw a dog out in public we'd make subtle commentary to each other ("appears to be a mutt";

"following leash instructions well"; "a bit nippy"). I'd longed to have a dog for years, but held off because I knew we didn't have the space, time, or money to care for one. Finding an apartment to rent with a dog in tow is nearly impossible; we didn't have the money for a dog when we'd lived in our basement apartment; and while I was in grad school, we didn't have the time to devote to dog rearing. We'd researched breeds exhaustively as a way to close the gap between the years we'd have to wait before our lives could support another being. And the time was now.

I saw dog ownership as another indicator of adulthood. Since I'd checked off "finish grad school" and "buy a house" this month, I figured we might as well check off "adopt a dog" too. Adulthood was all going to happen for me during the month of August 2012. We'd settled on adopting a greyhound several years before, since our research (both in the field and through compulsively taking "What's My Dream Pup?" quizzes online) indicated this was the ideal breed for us because they don't need a lot of space or exercise, they typically don't bark, drool, or shed much, and they're content to laze around the house all day. Plus, they're equal parts frugal and humanitarian since they're rescues from the racetrack—no expensive breeder to pay, and they're adult dogs so no need to enroll them in doggie daycare, which in Cambridge are as prevalent (and probably as expensive) as human child daycare. We'd even picked out a name, Gracie, and on August 16, a dainty, copper-colored greyhound, who looked more like a small deer than a dog, joined our family. This was it. After years of waiting and planning, of mistakenly thinking I'd made it, my adulthood was finally coming into focus. Happiness unlocked, or so I hoped.

6

Our Watershed Coffee Shop Conversation: A Dream Is Hatched

It was Saturday, March 29, 2014, and I was looking at our reflection in the coffee shop's front window while bending down to drink, without hands, from my overfull, steaming latte. Nate had the early scruff of a beard and my short nails, on long-fingered hands gripping my knees, were painted dark purple. I was wearing $285 leather boots; Nate had on skinny jeans. While I sat staring at the people city life had transformed us into, Nate was unspooling a mental blueprint for a radically different existence. Starting from the premise that we're both happiest when we're hiking in the woods, Nate drew the obvious, but previously taboo, conclusion that we should find a way to spend a larger percentage of our time in the woods. Namely, by moving there.

Nate and I'd had many versions of this conversation since we'd started hiking, usually on mountaintops. But this Saturday in March it was no longer the half-baked follow-your-dreams bluster of a college sophomore deciding to study surfboard construction in Indonesia in order to "find myself." Nate had been tinkering with our financial projections, and shared his findings using his fingers to enumerate each idea. First, he said, pointing at me with his thumb, we have a pretty high combined income. I nodded. Second—his pointer finger stabbed the espresso-redolent air—we've been saving at the fairly high rate of 40 to 50 percent of our take-home pay every month, not including our 401(k) contributions and mortgage principal. I was listening. What he'd figured out was that if we ramped up our savings rate and maintained our incomes for several years—he estimated three years and five months (you know, roughly)—we'd have enough money to move to a homestead in the woods-filled countryside of Vermont, rent out our Cambridge house, and get lower-paying jobs. Or better yet, no jobs at all. Nate was rhapsodizing in a way wholly divorced from his standard engineer's economy of spoken word. At that point, I think I would've agreed to anything that would break us out of our entrenched corporate routines. In the last year, it'd become obvious that Nate and I were repeating a failing pattern: we'd move to a new city, get new jobs, and expect different results. But with each move and each new first day of work came higher and higher expectations coupled with less and less patience for life to start clicking. We hadn't been back in Cambridge for even two years yet, and I'd already suffered the paralyzing realization that I'd likely never feel adequately fulfilled or happy, or whatever it is you feel when you're living the life you're meant to live. It just wasn't going to happen for me via my well-paying but ultimately energy-sucking nine-to-five cubicle job. Didn't matter the job; didn't matter the city; didn't matter the house we owned; didn't matter the dog we'd adopted. We were both, without a doubt, unhappy.

We walked home from the coffee shop holding hands, not talking. Nate had exhausted his voice having spoken more words than is normal for him in about a week, and my face was on fire with brain overwork. I felt like I'd just woken up from a late afternoon nap, hazy from dreams and stunned by the realization that it wasn't morning. I needed cold water. We canceled our plans to go out to dinner that night and instead ate frozen pizza while poring over the spreadsheets Nate had assembled with projections ranging from how much money we could save each month to what we could charge in rent for our Cambridge home to purchase prices for rural properties to standard stock market returns for our portfolio of low-fee index funds. Midway through dinner, I told Nate it was a go. After four hours of hearing him talk with more passion than I'd heard from him in the last seven years, I knew there was no way we could zip this dream back up. It was out like an air mattress, expanding by the minute, never to be stuffed neatly into its factory-issued carrying case ever again.

I was breathless about this novel life path, but I had a nagging feeling that, in a way, I'd failed. At twenty-two, I was consumed with crafting a meticulous career. And I'd done it. Now, at thirty, I was preparing to abandon everything I'd worked for in favor of, let's be honest, a pretty bizarre idea. I didn't know anyone who'd opted out of conventional success. Was this even allowed? Despite my confidence in Nate and in the math, I was unsettled by my own compulsion to follow the rules. I knew there was no way I could've embraced this path right after college because I was obsessed with traditional metrics of success then. But I felt so let down by the conformist path I'd followed up to this point that I was willing to take a leap. I was starting to accept that for me, fulfillment didn't come in a paycheck envelope. I'd done everything you're "supposed" to do. And I hated it. The idea of not having a pat answer to the question, "What do you do for work?" had haunted me for years. Now, I was ready to move out from underneath these constraints I'd imposed on myself.

Nate and I don't fester in unhappiness and we don't abide regrets, as we kept proving to ourselves by moving every few years. When we want something different, we act on it. For approximately three minutes that evening, we discussed moving to the country immediately, but we both knew that wasn't the right choice for two research-driven, cautious people who won't even leave the house without bringing water bottles and snacks, no matter where we're going. Girded by pages of spreadsheet machinations, Nate and I agreed on the strategic, decisive three-year, five-month timeline to allow us to save up enough money and prepare ourselves to blow up our lives. Starting the process right away was the only thing that made sense to us. There'd be no delaying until the following week or until our next paychecks; we started that night. And we never looked back.

As it turned out, the financial elements and their corresponding timeline weren't the totality of Nate's plan. Nate already knew that his interests were fully incorporated into his projections. For his entire life, he's wanted to be some sort of modern-day mountain man/lumberjack/hiker/engineer out in the wilderness. When he was a toddler, his grandparents called him the little man, and in high school, his parents couldn't stop him from going on solo camping trips and storm-chasing tornadoes by himself through the Kansas prairies. He was born with a desire for solitude, self-sufficiency, and nature. I, on the other hand, was a convert to the whole woods thing, and while it's true I love to hike, we weren't going to hike together all day every day. Nate thought I needed a vocation to lure me into a remote corner of a mostly wooded state with a smaller population than our neighborhood in Cambridge. In his mind, in order for this to work, I had to be impassioned. And so, Nate divulged that he'd bought me something: a domain name. For a blog. That he'd already set up and designed.

He beamed while explaining that it was just *waiting* for me to write something. I was furious, to put it mildly.

Being told what to do, even by the person who usually knows me better than I know myself, rankled my independent core. I told Nate I didn't appreciate that he'd presumed to know what I needed and that I would've liked to be privy to this little decision of his. But Nate already knew this too, and that if he'd left it up to me, I would've spent five months dithering over a name for the blog, and another two years second-guessing whether or not I was a good enough writer to type something into a computer and hit "publish," subjecting myself to the harsh, erratic judgment of the Internet. He'd taken a gamble that he could backdoor me into writing by making me feel that I'd be hurting his feelings, not to mention wasting the time and money he'd invested in the site already. He was banking on my obstinate hatred of frittering away sunk costs. And he was right. Sometimes it takes the perspective of an outsider (even if it's just your own spouse) to tell you what you need the most.

Back in college when I decided to change my major to English, my true passion, I was worried that creative writing wasn't employable-sounding. To combat this, I tacked on a more employable-sounding double major in political science, because all of my friends, Nate included, were majoring in it. In the eight years since graduation, I'd barely written a creative word. I'd labored over a few atrocious short stories that I hope are irretrievably lost somewhere on my computer, lest I die and someone actually read them. And of course, I'd hacked out my grad school coursework in Cheetos-fueled frenzies along with countless unread thank-you letters from the confines of my varying shades of gray cubicles. Nate and I had two failed blogs already—one about public transit, which never got beyond being something we talked about after two glasses of wine—and an anemic, dull rendering of navigating life in Cambridge. Given this lusterless résumé, I wasn't optimistic for an oddly named blog about what I viewed as the *most* uninteresting thing about me: my frugality. Prepared for my rebuttals, Nate flung me another motivator: we'd have to explain the whole situation to our families, and we both knew it would come across more coherently and less like we'd lost our minds if I wrote it out. I couldn't disagree there. After listening to me bemoan my failure to write for years, Nate decided I needed to be forced/encouraged into, well, writing something. The morning after we decided to have a really early midlife crisis together, I stared at the empty WordPress website Nate had named Frugalwoods. If you'd asked me to think of a more lunatic moniker, I could not have; but I trusted Nate's instincts. I used to pick at Nate's nonconformity, haranguing him for his refusal to wear khaki pants and button-down shirts like everyone else. His sense of the offbeat is on point, and I think the offbeat is what populates the cubbyholes of the Internet.

To get me over my crippling fear of bad writing, Nate assured me that nobody would read the blog. I decided to write anonymously, mostly so I could disavow having ever written it if it was terrible (which my neurosis and perfectionism assured me it would be). Thusly coddled, I started writing. And Nate was right; I did know frugality. It was how I'd made it through college with no debt, lived in New York City for a year on $8,000, and bought a house at age twenty-eight. But I'd never tried to explain it to anyone else before. Once I started writing, it flowed like the release of steam from a pressurized cannon. I could not stop. I published my first post on April 9, 2014, and nearly four years later, I haven't run out of words yet.

7

Our First Month of Extreme Frugality

After Nate and I bought our house in the summer of 2012, I felt compelled to fill it up with furniture. This was our first real home and empty rooms (plus a card table) just wouldn't do. We bought a king-size knock-off memory foam mattress on Amazon for $279 and, studiously following the instructions to "open only in the room where it will reside," unfurled it atop our similarly cheap bedframe. It sprung to life like one of those pill-shaped pellets that expands into an animal-shaped sponge when dropped into water, which I'd beg my mom to buy in the checkout line at the grocery store when I was a kid. I had no clue if a $279 knock-off king-size memory foam mattress from Amazon would be any good, or if it would last, or have any attributes resembling comfort, but for that price—as opposed to the brand-name price tag of over $2,000—it was worth the frugal gamble. And since I know how this story ends, I can tell you that nearly six years later our $279 knock-off memory foam mattress remains remarkably comfortable, has survived a move, and is still mattressing on. But that mattress took care of only one room in our otherwise empty house.

In one of our quests for house filler, we double-parked our seventeen-year-old Honda Odyssey minivan, which was badly dented along its entire left side and defaced with a stripe of green paint where I'd interacted with a pillar of the same hue in the American University parking garage a few years back. The van now questionably parked, Nate and I ran up the three stories of a Boston brownstone that we hoped contained our future couch. I refused to buy new furniture (with the exception of our knock-off mattress) for our mostly empty house, on the premise that it was ridiculous to pay full price when I could find used items on Craigslist (or at garage sales or on the side of the road) for at least 75 percent less. After learning the exact height of our minivan while trying to shove a too-tall couch in there one afternoon, and then learning the precise width of our front door in a similar operation, I now knew to ask sellers for exact dimensions. And this couch? Up these three flights of stairs? It was exactly the right size.

The sellers opened their front door and I was surprised they were my age, because I didn't think people my age had any furniture to sell yet. I mean, how long could they have possibly owned this stuff? Five years, tops? Newly-weds, they explained they were "of course" buying all new furniture now that they were married. Nate and I declined to mention that we'd been married for four years and were just now buying our first couch, used, from them. I asked if they had any other stuff they were selling and sure enough, the bride wanted her husband's leather armchair gone. We offered them $250 for both and they bit. I was thrilled they were getting rid of a couch that looked, felt, and smelled perfectly fine (it was trendy, even) and an all-leather chair that, I checked, originally retailed for $950. Nate and I inexpertly levered the couch over our heads in order to clear the antique banister in the elevatorless building. We hustled it down to our double-parked minivan and discovered we'd be paying another $50 in the form of a parking ticket. Since both couch and chair wouldn't squeeze into the van together (I mean, there are limits, even in a minivan with all of its backseats removed), we drove the couch home to Cambridge, unloaded it into our living room, and bolted back for the chair.

My commitment to the secondhand market deepened as I witnessed firsthand the remarkable depreciation curve that new furniture undergoes in its spiral down to the nominal prices I paid for it on Craigslist with my envelope of cash. New stuff—cars, clothing, furniture—is usually not an investment, meaning that except in *rare* circumstances, it does not appreciate. It's easy to trick ourselves into thinking we'll buy something for life, or invest in a couch that'll hold its value for decades, but that resale moment rarely comes to fruition.

Being a person who owns a $285 pair of leather boots, I keenly understand the desire to pay for quality and to subscribe to the idea that I'll never buy another pair of boots in my entire life. But how often does this actually pan out? We (I include myself here) get bored with our stuff. Our style and tastes change. We move houses and need a bigger/smaller/more purple couch. This notion that we can future-proof our material possessions is, more often than not, a woeful excuse for overpaying. By instead embracing the used market, I was able to find higher-quality pieces of furniture for far less than their cheap, new, particleboard analogues. Same goes for clothes. The brand names I source from thrift stores are typically better made and more stylish than new and inexpensive fast-fashion outfits intended to be worn and thrown out in the course of a single season. After I slowly outfitted our entire home via the used market for a total sum of $1,000, I was a diehard convert to the world of secondhand.

I'd scour the Craigslist furniture section early every Saturday morning and email anything that seemed promising, requesting (exact) dimensions and directions. I learned to always ask people what else they were selling because people are always selling more than one thing and you can usually get a bundled deal a la my couch-n-chair combo. And I always offered less than asking price, which *almost* always worked. After each successful cheap purchase, in a fit of hypocrisy, to celebrate finding an end table for $5 and a dresser for $20, Nate and I would go out to dinner at Lord Hobo or Atwood's or any number of other superb Cambridge eateries. The irony that we were spending upward of $50 on our celebratory meal was lost on us at the time. In our early days of home ownership, frugality appealed to me when it was a contest and when I could find deals and barter with sellers.

Now, two years later and two days after launching our move-to-the-woods plan, I was coming face-to-face with the fiscal ramifications of all those celebratory meals. Nate and I sat staring at his laptop on our wide wooden plank dining room table, which we'd bought for $75, including the four woven cloth chairs, from a Scandinavian couple who'd moved it into their thirty-foot-ceiling Boston loft all the way from Scandinavia and then decided it didn't work in their new concrete-floored home. Nate opened a spreadsheet he'd exported from our bank account detailing every dollar we'd spent the previous month, which we hadn't known would be our last month ever pre-extreme frugality. The first element of our plan was that we needed to save more money. Full stop. I'd thought we *were* frugal and smart with our money, sitting as we were at this discounted table and chairs in a home we owned to which respectable-size paychecks were delivered. But I'd never tested this theory, and I'd never actually combed through every dollar we spent in a month. Kind of a painful process the first time you do it, let me tell you.

Once I started earning a decent income, and then most especially after Nate's similarly decent salary was stacked on top of mine in the melting pot of our marital bank accounts, we stopped micromanaging our spending. By which I mean I had no clue what we spent in any given week, month, or year. Back in my Brooklyn AmeriCorps days, I counted every bar of soap I bought for fear I'd overdraw my account. All I'd wanted then was to have enough money to not have to deliberate for weeks over whether to spend $10 on a grocery cart to tote my clothes to and from the laundromat. Now that I'd experienced a life of spending $40 a week on artisanal cheeses and $120 on haircuts and $200 on dinners out, I realized it wasn't what I wanted. What was the point of being able to buy whatever I wanted if I didn't control my *time*? I'd thought money was the ultimate resource, but it was dawning on me that time is actually the greatest resource of all. More specifically, the ability to use my time as I wished. It wasn't that I hated my job, I didn't; it's that I spent too many hours there, marooned in a cubicle, with my tasks dictated by other people, unable to work on things I felt inspired by.

Staring at what seemed like unfathomable dollar amounts on this blindingly white spreadsheet tallying our March 2014 expenses, I understood that Nate and I had fallen for the most hackneyed trope of the American dream: we were spending more and more money in increasingly desperate attempts to mitigate the frustration and discontent we felt over our jobs. We were working for the weekends and spending the money we'd worked so hard to earn in an effort to make ourselves feel better about how hard we worked. It was a vicious cycle. We were firmly entrenched at that point. After reaching the mammoth goal of buying our house, we entered what I now call a period of financial purgatory: we'd failed to map out a next step for our money. Buying our house had been *it*, the only thing we'd planned for. There was no next goal. Until now. Those two goalless years reared up on Nate's spreadsheet graphs like volcanoes we'd stupidly thought were dormant and were now trying to summit, wondering why molten earth was coursing around our feet. We'd drifted through these two years as mindless consumers, convincing ourselves that we needed, nay *deserved*, new iPhones and wall art.

In the aftermath of closing on our house, we'd gone out to eat maybe once a week. But then we started to think, *If it's nice to eat out once a week, wouldn't it be even nicer to get takeout another night, and nicer still to get lattes and scones every Saturday afternoon?* What I didn't know at the time is that Nate and I were victims of the hedonic adaptation that plagues our consumption-focused society. Hedonic adaptation is the concept that we calibrate ourselves to whatever we repeatedly do. If we constantly reward or treat ourselves (with restaurants and scones), we deaden our ability to derive true pleasure from those rewards. Then we require larger and more frequent rewards.

It's also a question of habit. We can acclimate ourselves to just about any level of expenditure or pleasure. After all, the superrich can't fathom how anyone survives without ten homes and five yachts. And sure, owning ten homes and five yachts sounds ridiculous, but is it *really* that much more ridiculous than wanting to eat at a restaurant every night of the week? In both situations, we're relying upon external forces to bring us happiness. In both situations, we're trading money for experiences, which we think will yield that ephemeral "good life." The problem is that when we get into the routine of trading money in order to make ourselves happy, we lose sight of any other routes to happiness. Like an addict, we start turning to money to solve more and more of our problems and to farm out more and more of our dissatisfaction with the life we've created and which we now must pay for. We become desensitized to pleasure and lose our capacity to experience joy from things we'd previously considered luxurious, such as a single restaurant meal a month. Nate and I realized we needed to disrupt this cycle of hedonic adaptation and recalibrate what brought us joy.

Looking at every dollar we spent in a regular old month—not even a month when something noteworthy, like a friend's wedding, happened—I felt like I do in the spring when I put on my bathing suit for the first time: exposed and larger than I had hoped. I was angry at myself. How had I let this lifestyle inflation happen? I'd considered myself a consummate frugalist. Yet here was irrefutable evidence of Nate and me flushing thousands of dollars down the drain on craft beer and throw pillows. I was tempted to tally up how much we could've saved if we'd been on a legit frugal path from the beginning, and if we'd known all along we were going to abandon the conventional life we'd originally forged.

But in the same breath, I knew that was impossible. I came around to this plan *because* of my firsthand experience with what it feels like to work forty hours a week and to spend all the money I wanted, not in spite of it. These past few years had been our spending Rumspringa; it was only through trying on the lifestyle of a typical American consumer that we were able to discern it wasn't for us. There would be no woods plan without first having this city spending plan. The money we'd spent wasn't wasted. Rather, it was sacrificed in service of figuring out what we wanted to do with our lives. Or at least, that's what I like to tell myself. Instead of wallowing in regret over these lost funds, I moved forward. I termed it our era of "start now and don't look back." Nate had done all manner of fancy spreadsheet calculations on how much money we could save and invest each month, and thus how quickly we could reach financial independence, but now it was time to see if his predictions were right.

Our watershed coffee shop conversation was on March 29, 2014, and so the month of April 2014 was our test drive in true extreme frugality. Our month to find out how little we could spend and still survive. Up to this point, we'd been Christmas and Easter frugalists, dipping in and out of fiscal prudence where it suited us, saving enough to ensure ourselves a spot in retirement, but also buying things like a handcrafted turquoise-and-brown embroidered collar for Gracie with a matching leash. It was time to renew our commitment. We enacted what we called our $0 budget. I've always thought that spending is like a gas: it expands to fill whatever space you allot to it. If we'd given ourselves a $1,000 monthly spending cap, I can almost guarantee we'd spend exactly $1,000. If we were at $990.01 on the last day of the month, we'd go buy a dog toy for $9.99 to make it even. My rationale was that with a $0 budget, I'd approach the month from the mind-set that I wasn't going to spend any money. At all. Obviously, I knew we'd have to buy stuff, but I'd consider every dollar spent as a debit against that paragon zero.

We decided that this most frugal month ever would have a twofold goal: 1) to see how much money we could save and 2) to test out how sustainable extreme frugality felt to us. Could we actually embrace living on less for the long term? Neither of us wanted to sell all of our possessions and go live in a yurt, but we also felt lied to by our "treat your-self" culture that parrots consumption as the cure for what ails. We needed to find a tenable middle ground between dumpster diving for our food and embracing the rampant, gratuitous spending that's considered normal and even necessary in our culture. Since most budgeting programs are based around the premise of bumping their acolytes up from a 0 percent savings rate to a 5 or 10 percent rate, and Nate and I were angling to boost what was already a 45 to 50 percent savings rate, we decided to strike out and create our own system.

In making the decision to ignore everything our culture said about money (that it's to be spent) and careers (that you must work them for over forty years), we had the somewhat alarming realization that there aren't very many people who do this sort of thing. This was a wholesale reckoning of how we used our money, how we viewed our consumption, what constituted a need for us, and how we structured our lives. We needed to identify where every dollar was going and either eliminate the expense, reduce it, or find a cheaper substitute.

Looking at our previous month's expenses was ideal because it gave us a baseline starting point. Trying to estimate what you spend in a month is a lot like the weight you tell yourself you are: much lower than reality. Better to step on the scale and face the real number. If we didn't know how much we were spending and what we were spending it on, there'd be no way to calibrate our projections. Sitting at our kitchen table, we divided our expenses into two categories: fixed and discretionary. Fixed costs are things that aren't easily changed. Our list included just one item:

our mortgage. Most budget gurus will shovel gigantic piles of expenses into the fixed section, including the likes of utilities, transportation, and groceries. But those things aren't actually fixed; they're calibrated upon our actions. If we choose to drive to work every day as opposed to taking public transportation or riding a bike, that's a decision we're making with a very real financial consequence. If we choose to turn the heat in our home up to 75 degrees in the wintertime, that's a choice with expensive repercussions. If we spend thousands of dollars every month on pricey prepackaged groceries, that again is a choice. I set aside our one fixed cost since we wouldn't be changing that quite yet, but I didn't forget about it. I now turned my attention to the yawning fissure of line item after line item of discretionary expenses. Lucky for me, there was a lot of low-hanging, overripe spending fruit for us to pick off that first month, a truism for just about everyone who performs this kind of audit.

Goaded on by my new infatuation with frugality, I busted out the delete key for every line item that wasn't a strict necessity. My litmus was: "Do we require this for our survival as two human people and one dog-child?" This is how we said goodbye to the unnecessary tchotchkes of city life: dining out, coffee shops, dry cleaning, cabs, bars, cafés, and takeout (OK, yes, a lot of it was food-related . . .). We already had a nearly nonexistent entertainment budget because things like paying double digits to sit in a dark room with a bunch of strangers to watch a program that you can't change the channel on if it's bad, and where you can't bring your own food, or put your feet up, or cuddle, or go to the bathroom any time you'd like, sounds more like a form of torture than entertainment to me. Suffice it to say, we watched movies at home. Nate and I had cultivated a lot of free hobbies over the years, such as walking, hiking, and cooking, thanks to our initial poverty and then our house-buying goal. All of these pursuits yielded major frugality dividends. I'm also averse on principle to paying for entertainment as it seems like a cop-out to me. Half of the fun is the quest and the creativity inherent in finding free or cheap stuff to do: cruising through free festivals and outdoor markets, going to museums on free-to-the-public days, reading books and magazines from the library, hosting friends for themed dinner parties, trying out fancy recipes at home. This philosophy of creating our own entertainment was already an ingrained aspect of our lives.

Next on my ruthless expense-chopping block, I decided to abolish the modern-day construct of paying other people to do things for us. This wasn't a super-huge category since we're insourcers by nature, but there was still room for improvement. We like the self-reliance, the collaboration, and the auxiliary benefit of learning new skills that results from embracing a wholly DIY existence. We'd refinished our kitchen cabinets ourselves, refurbished our staircase, painted walls, and done a smattering of other renovations in our house. We washed our own dog and cleaned our own home. Our only outsourced activity at the time were our haircuts, which we decided we could handle in-house.

Next up were things crucial to our basic survival, but that weren't fixed costs, a category that included groceries, household supplies like toilet paper, dog food, clothing, and our utility bills (water and electricity). The goal here was to reduce the amount we spent in each of these categories. I'd always glossed over grocery costs in the past with the glib assumption that since food is a necessity, I didn't need to think about how much I was spending. But I was out $40 a week in the artisanal cheese section alone before I even got to the chocolate-covered sea-salt raspberries and the sparkling white wine. I needed to find less expensive alternatives and learn how to compare price per square foot of toilet paper (and price per ounce of almonds, and per pound of apples . . .). It wasn't about decreasing the quality of our food, but rather about being conscious of what things cost and how to achieve the same end result—a healthy diet—for less.

After making these eliminations, we were left with a small, but crucial, list. These were the things we didn't want to give up. These were the items and the experiences that we felt added significant value to our lives. In order to retain this value in our lives, we decided to find frugal substitutions for each.

I didn't view this new and intense level of frugality as a

mechanism of deprivation, I instead saw it as an opportunity to identify my priorities. I wanted to isolate the variables that constituted my core happiness. My goal was to figure out when spending money made actionable, appreciable difference in my life, versus when spending money was superfluous, unimportant, and beyond the scope of what brought me lasting enjoyment.

A lot of my spending had become automatic, mindless swipes of the credit card that I repeatedly did out of sheer habit. Enter my Dunkin' Donuts routine. I used to buy an iced tea from Dunkin' Donuts almost every single weekday afternoon with my best work buddy, Jess, not because I liked the iced tea, as it's actually horrendous-tasting, but because I wanted to spend time with my friend. It dawned on me that she and I could just as easily enjoy a walk together instead of a trek over to Dunkin' Donuts. We could catch up on our work gossip, stretch our legs, and get out of our cubicles for a few minutes without the accompanying loss of $2.50 per day. Easy. Stripping away pointless purchases like this unneeded and unwanted iced tea helped me to identify priorities—in this case, quality time with my friend—and divorce them from spending money. All I had to do in order to save hundreds of dollars every month was bring consciousness to my daily transactions.

I also reasoned that if I could get all of our furniture for a fraction of the price by substituting Craigslist for swanky furniture stores, there had to be frugal analogues for lots of other things too. We could've entirely eliminated every single line item not required for human survival from our budget, but Nate and I were angling for long-term sustainability in our frugality. We once did the South Beach Diet together, which was not the greatest of ideas we've ever had. We stuck to it like some hardcore mofos for about a month (full disclosure: it did work in helping us both lose weight), but we were miserable. Mis-er-a-ble. We bailed on it in favor of a more moderate but wholesale transformation of how we eat. We made our long-term diet sustainable by allowing for treats and the stuff we love eating (except for Cheetos, as I have a certified problem with Cheetos and had to quit those full stop). The same approach was effective with our frugality. By retaining the things we love, we were able to craft a lifestyle that isn't focused solely on saving money, but rather, on optimizing for our priorities. Your priorities are surely different than mine, but by allowing this principle to guide your budgeting process, I imagine you'll be amazed at how many insignificant line items are gobbling up your funds month after month. The key is to identify what matters most to you, what brings you the deepest enjoyment, and then abolish all of the subpar iced teas on which you're frittering away your cash.

The biggest-ticket line item that I did *not* want to give up were my yoga classes. For several years, I'd been taking yoga two or three nights a week, and every Saturday morning, with Nate at a heated power-yoga studio a few blocks from our house. They were a priority; I loved both the classes and the community, and regular yoga had whipped me into the best physical shape of my life. But I was spending $18 on *each and every class*, which tallied up to a whopping $288 per month. Ouch. There was no way that $3,456 per year on yoga fit into a regime of extreme frugality. I was bummed. While sulking about this sacrifice, I remembered a poster hanging up in my studio that read "Do you want free yoga classes?" in purple letters across the top. And I thought, *Why yes, in fact, that's exactly what I want.* There was no excuse (none whatsoever) for the fact that I'd never paid attention to this poster before, but it was a perfect illustration of how myopic I'd been in my presumed frugality. Two days later, I was sitting behind the front desk being trained as a yoga studio assistant. I felt like a world-class idiot for the thousands, *thousands* of dollars I'd spent on classes over the years when I could've been getting them for free. Never mind that, no time for regrets. I learned how to navigate the computer system (turns out, there's a whole suite of software just for yoga studios), how to run the credit card machine, how to mop the studio, and how to take out the trash after class. I'd discovered the wonderful world of barter and trade, which my modern cultural training had informed me was dead. False, I learned as I asked, "How would you like to pay for class this evening?" and then rolled out my mat for free.

My newfound understanding of the role of barter and

trade in our modern economy served me well as I frugalized every aspect of my life. I'd always considered it an
antiquated concept with no presence in our market economy, but how wrong I was. In the years since uncovering
this magical free yoga hack, I've heard from folks all around
the world who have a similar barter and trade arrangement
with their yoga/ballet/Pilates/CrossFit studio/gym/pool. The
opportunities to trade your time are available; you just
have to seek them out.

After combing through our entire rundown of expenses
and striking off restaurants and new clothes and haircuts
with barely a hesitation of the delete key, I landed on another luxury I didn't want to sacrifice: seltzer water. Yes,
I said seltzer water. Nate and I are bubbly-water fanatics
because it's how we both quit drinking soda. I crave car-
bonation more than the ersatz flavors of soda, so seltzer
was my deliverance from both the expense and the health
detriments of fizzy pop. We don't add syrups or flavors to
our seltzer, so it's just plain old H_2O; however, the inserts
for our SodaStream seltzer machine still cost money. Quite
a bit of money, as it turned out. Nate and I were drinking
a whopping 180 liters of seltzer per month, which, in case
you're wondering, required that we purchase three Soda-
Stream CO_2 inserts a month at the rate of $15 a pop. Don't
worry, I'll do the math for you: that's $45 per month and
a staggering $540 per year on bubbly water. This had to
change. Since seltzer was one of our identified priorities

(don't laugh, everyone's priorities are different . . .) we realized we'd have to devise a frugal alternative.

Ever the industrious frugal DIY-er, Nate figured out a way to hack our SodaStream machine to hook it up to a gigantic (OK, just twenty-pound) CO_2 tank, which meant our fizzy water now cost something like half a penny per serving as opposed to the $540 per year we were spending on SodaStream inserts. A twenty-pound tank of CO_2 cost $35 and, since we used roughly two tanks annually, we were on track to save $470 per year. Sure, it would've been cheapest to simply do away with our bubbles entirely, but we wanted to embrace a lifestyle of luxurious frugality. A lifestyle where we were saving an inordinately high percentage of our incomes, but also enjoying life. Since this was a quest to create a life we truly loved, we saw no point in making ourselves miserable in the process.

These types of frugal substitutions and alternatives were all around us. We marveled at everything we'd been unwittingly overpaying for. By bringing creativity and ingenuity to our consumption, we were able to drastically reduce our overall spending. I'll grant you that $470 might not sound like a whole lot of money to save, but what you have to remember is that once you eliminate an expense, you've eliminated it forever. It's not that we were saving a mere $470 in one year, we were saving $470 every year for the rest of our lives (or at least, until we stop drinking seltzer, which I imagine will be after we're dead). Plus, all of our savings were stacked one on top of the other, which is how you create an extremely frugal lifestyle. We weren't saving just $470 on seltzer per year, we were saving $470 plus the $3,456 on yoga plus $1,008 on haircuts . . . and on and on and on until we were saving thousands upon thousands of dollars every single year. Forever.

There's a theory in behavioral economics related to loss aversion positing that once we acclimate to a certain level of luxury or ownership in our lives—be it seltzer or expensive yoga classes—we find it nearly impossible to then live without this luxury. Giving these things up feels like deprivation because we've acclimated ourselves to their presence in our lives. Knowing this, and knowing that we wanted to sustain a lower cost of living forever, Nate and I put a lot of time and effort into devising our frugal workarounds. I don't think the route to successful frugality entails brutally slashing everything from your budget, because you're bound to end up in that deprived state that behavioral economists have documented. Rather, the key is to identify less expensive options that'll yield the same or a similar end result. Thus, you end up not feeling deprived, you save a boatload of money, and you are motivated to find even more opportunities for dramatic changes and the resulting savings. Once you begin down the road of frugalizing, it's nearly impossible to stop. It becomes a game, a competition, and an invigorating challenge. You get to win at your own life.

In the unfurling of this personal frugality boot camp, Nate and I made the discovery that we were both second-marshmallow kids. Not literally, as we weren't lucky enough to be actual subjects in this research experiment, but we fall into a category of people wired from an early age for delayed gratification. You've probably heard of what's often referred to as the Stanford marshmallow study of the '60s and '70s, in which preschoolers underwent a now-classic test in delayed gratification. In this experiment, researchers sat a preschooler at a desk alone in a room, with two marshmallows atop the desk and the following instructions: the researcher needed to leave the room for a moment and the child could either eat one marshmallow while the researcher was absent or, if the child could wait until the researcher returned, the child could eat both marshmallows. Some of the kids are like, "hey, bird in the hand!" and gobble one 'mallow. But other, weirder kids, like me and Nate, agonizingly wait for the researcher to return in order to savor the promised, greater prize of two marshmallows.

When I was in second grade, my teacher gave us coupons for good behavior that we could redeem for prizes. There were pencils and erasers you could get for five coupons, a rubber ball for ten coupons, and other nominal kid trinkets for each increment of coupons saved. At the very top of the prize bookshelf, there was a row of stuffed animals that were redeemable for one hundred coupons each. One hundred coupons is a lot of good behavior. One hundred coupons is *months'* worth of listening, walking in line, raising your hand, being a good friend, not cutting people with scissors, and turning your work in on time. I had my eye on a Care Bear on that top shelf, Tenderheart Bear to be precise, and I watched Tenderheart Bear all year long. I studied her (his? gender was never clear . . .) beaming bear smile and the big red heart stitched on her chest. Every time I collected a coupon, for not eating glue and for remembering my permission slip, I stole a glance at Tenderheart Bear, planning, plotting, waiting. In May 1992, which was the final month of my second-grade career, I had one hundred coupons at last. I got to take Tenderheart Bear home with me. She was covered in dust because, as my teacher explained to my mom, those big stuffed animals had been sitting up on that top shelf for years.

I don't know why Nate and I are both so attuned to the merits of delayed gratification, but it's an attribute we've brought out and enhanced in each other. Sacrificing short-term desires like lattes and scones on Saturday afternoons for the long-term gains of living life on our own terms makes rational sense to both of us. It also appeals to our ingrained desire for efficiency. We both recognized that the pleasure we'd derive from those weekly dopamine (not to mention sugar) hits of our latte treats couldn't compete with the promise of not having to slump in grayscale cubicles every Monday through every Friday for nearly every year of our adult lives. Since we were working toward an ever-crystallizing goal of decamping to the woods, frugality wasn't about what we were giving up; it was entirely about what we were going to gain.

8

Less Makeup, More Confidence

I figured out that if I put my makeup on while riding the number 64 bus into work, I could sleep an extra ten minutes every morning. After stabbing myself in the eyeball with mascara, I learned to wait for red lights. I started to exaggerate my snooze button usage and cut it closer and closer, to the point where I had fifteen minutes between crawling out of bed and sprinting to the bus stop five blocks away at an unassuming spot on the sidewalk in Central Square, Cambridge, between the India Pavilion and Falafel Palace restaurants. One morning I climbed onto the bus out of breath, owing to the fact that as I came down the sidewalk, I'd seen the number 64 sitting at the red light before my stop and bolted to intercept the bus so that I wouldn't have to wait twenty minutes for the next one. I sank into a seat near the back, frustrated with my job and this rushed, ridiculous routine to get to my desk every day by 9 a.m. I pawed around in my purse, absentmindedly at first, then with growing franticness, and then took everything out slowly, one item at a time, knowing but not wanting to accept that I'd forgotten my makeup bag. I leaned my head back onto the collar of my coat and moaned.

I considered getting off at the next stop and walking back home, grabbing my makeup bag, and then catching the next number 64 that was due in seventeen minutes. But I was frazzled and already late. So I came up with a plan. I got off the bus at work, walked across the street to the CVS drugstore, and bought $50 worth of moisturizer, powder, concealer, blush, eyeliner, eye shadow, mascara, and lipstick. I hauled my goods over to work and went into a bathroom not on my floor, hoping to avoid having one of my colleagues see me unwrap this pile of brand-new makeup and apply it right there at the bathroom sink while I was supposed to be in my cubicle. I hadn't considered going to work that day without makeup for even a moment.

Starting my freshman year of high school, I never went anywhere without makeup, because I harbored a deep-seated belief that something was wrong with the way I looked naturally. I thought my hair was either too oily or too dry or too full or too thin, and my skin was plagued with incidents, like old chicken pox scars, that I wanted to plaster over. At fourteen, I foresaw a lifetime of defects I'd have to fight against. It started with my acne and I figured that, soon enough, I'd need to combat wrinkles and gray hair. In my early twenties, I had an earnest conversation

with my friend Alisha about whether we should start using antiwrinkle cream under our eyes as a prophylactic. I'm
not sure where this self-loathing originated—whether from
beauty industry ads targeting every part of my body and that
seemed to prey on, and even create, insecurities in women,
or the popular girls at school who had this body-morphing
all figured out with their detailed makeup regimens and
magazine-worthy hair, or my own adolescent insecurities.
Whatever the case, I'd internalized the message that I
needed to fix myself. To change myself. I also began to
understand that women are expected to do everything: we
must be consummate careerists, doting mothers, and above
all else immaculately turned out, never mind the time,
money, and confidence this drains from us.

Lucky for me, the problems I perceived I had—and
plenty I hadn't even thought of before, like a commercial
that once induced me to go measure my eyelashes because
maybe they weren't long enough—could be solved with
money. All the natural inclinations of my body, its odors,
its tendency to grow hair in places other than the top of
my head, should be fought against. Furthermore, I should
be embarrassed if I didn't. It wasn't just the lip gloss ads in
Seventeen magazine that fanned my adolescent self-doubt;
it was other women too. I calibrated what I should do
based on them and felt I had no voice, no agency to break
away. Who was I to say that we women should abandon
shoes that cause bunions, and reclaim hours of our lives

spent straightening curly hair and curling straight hair? I signed up for this lifelong pursuit of an air-brushed, plasticized version of womanhood at fourteen and was a rapt consumer for the next sixteen years. I hated how I looked as a teenager, which was ironic considering that's when I looked *most* like this idealized version. I'd stand in front of the mirror and outline my flaws, ticking down a mental list I nurtured. I fantasized about somehow perfecting myself, of deleting fat and acne, of adding curves. I performed this self-defeating ritual until, I'm embarrassed to say, I was thirty years old. Not coincidentally, it was right about the time Nate and I embarked on our journey of extreme frugality. Since frugality caused me to identify all the areas where I was spending money in ways that were unfulfilling, it also caused me to identify all the areas where I was spending my time and energy in ways that were unfulfilling. Shaming my body on a daily basis? Decidedly unfulfilling, not to mention a waste of time and, very often, a waste of money as I searched out products to help remedy my bodily crisis of the day. I'd internalized negative messages about my appearance from an early age, but that was an old, worn-out battle that I could give up. Just like Dunkin' Donuts iced teas, I could eliminate this ugly obsession from my life. After this revelation, I never criticized my body again.

About six months after launching our new life as extreme frugality adherents, I noticed my concealer stick was running low. I scraped out the dregs of face-colored mud with my fingernail and smeared it as thinly as possible over my pimples. I'm plagued with lifelong acne, so at thirty, my face looked roughly the same as it had when I was sixteen, dotted with whiteheads and angry, red, mosquito-bite-size pimples. I raked through every drawer in my bathroom, hoping to find a sample concealer my mom had sent me from a Clinique gift set that she hadn't wanted. No luck. I searched online to see if I could sign up for free samples from somewhere, anywhere. I haunted drugstores hoping they'd discount their makeup at some point (they didn't).

Nate and I had obliterated all of our unnecessary expenses and were now spending under $1,000 a month on everything but our mortgage payment. I couldn't justify wasting money on makeup when we'd given up buying signed first-edition books through our local bookstore's first-edition club. I decided I wasn't someone who would forgo an inscribed Margaret Atwood in favor of a Maybelline concealer stick. It smacked of vacuousness. I was prying the last of my eye shadow out with a toothpick one morning when the absurdity of what I was doing dawned on me: Why wasn't I solving the root of this problem? Why didn't I just *stop wearing makeup*? The simple answer is that I thought I didn't look good without makeup. My self-worth was intertwined with my appearance. I was ashamed of my dependence on this stuff and of how difficult it was for me to even *consider* living without it.

Breaking away from traditional consumer norms as it related to my spending had opened my eyes to all the other ways in which I'd molded myself to fit cultural expectations. I didn't ever particularly enjoy the process of wearing makeup, but I'd also never considered stopping before. It wasn't until I had the experience of self-liberation from my previously mindless consumerism that I was able to reflect on my adherence to norms of other stripes. It was an entire process of me learning to let go of everything that wasn't deeply important to me as a person. Not to me as a person trying to impress others, or conform to a standard, or fit a stereotype, but to me on my own as an individual. I had my own voice, I could make my own decisions, and for the first time I was going to.

Acknowledging the presence of my addiction cemented my resolve to stop. I figured I'd take the same approach I do at the beach where I inch into cold waves one rung of my body at a time so that when the water laps at my shoulders, I'm fully acclimated and don't even realize I'm submerged. I'd eliminate one piece of makeup per week. First, I stopped painting my nails every Sunday afternoon. I felt like a peasant and spent the next Monday at work waiting for someone to comment on my bare, pedestrian nails. No one noticed. Next up, I didn't wear blush. Then, I eliminated powder. The following week, concealer was gone. It took me an entire month to phase everything out. Last to go was supposed to be mascara, but I couldn't do it. It stayed on as my security blanket against a naked, revealed face. But the concealer, the blush, the powder, the eye shadow, the eyeliner, the nail polish, and the lipstick? All gone. I thought I looked anemic and a touch Amish. I'd become more accustomed to my fake, made-up face than my actual, natural face. I'd embodied the prescribed societal standards of beauty to such an extent that I saw my makeup-less face as a failure. At the same time, I was invigorated the first day I went to work without makeup. I felt like I'd accomplished something, like I'd vanquished an old foe that'd dogged me for years, hanging over my shoulder whispering, "You're not good enough" in my ear. I'd thrown off this tormenter and it made me feel powerful. If I could do this, what else could I achieve? This wasn't the achievement of my old life, of my persistent, unhappy drive for external accolades; this was an achievement just for me. No one else would notice or care, but I would know. I would care. I would feel better.

Not wearing makeup didn't change my relationships. I was no more or less liked and I was no more or less successful. All those years I'd wasted so much time stressing out over what people thought about my ability to apply eyeliner, when in reality they didn't even notice. My feminist interior monologue, which'd been running since I was five years old and told my parents I didn't want to go to church unless women could be priests, was now written as a declaration of independence on my face. I wasn't going to do things that made me unhappy anymore, not with my money, not with my appearance, not with my life. I was gaining confidence in who I am at my core and what I look like without a veneer of self-imposed "shoulds" covering up my face and my actions.

Around this same time, I had a come-to-Jesus moment with my clothes because they were another ingredient in my lack of confidence. My conception of my self-worth started with my face and extended down to my shoes, and it ran only skin deep. I had way too much clothing. Way too much. After doing an inventory of my closet, I realized I could wear a different outfit every single day for two months straight. Wow. I bought clothes to treat myself, a habit my mother started me on when I was very young. We'd go shopping, always for sales, but without *needing* the stuff we came home with. I'd conflated the fact that a person needs to wear clothes with clothes being a "need." I was a thrift-store, garage-sale, and Kohl's clearance-rack hunter and I rarely spent more than $20 per item; even my red Banana Republic raincoat was just $18 from a high-end consignment shop in a ritzy suburb of Boston. I'd always thought I was so clever with these deals I found. But I'd missed the truism that every sale in the world won't save you as much money as simply not buying anything. Buying clothes didn't automatically make me more confident or more beautiful; it just automatically meant I had less money. Plus, clothing couldn't mask the fact that I was unhappy with how my life was unfolding. They were a smokescreen that I employed in an effort to appear polished, poised, and happy when, in reality, I felt the opposite. I reasoned that doing away with this camouflage would allow me to instead draw out my interior self.

I love winning so I was exhilarated with success over the forklifts of money we were saving every month. Frugality had become a competition that pitted us against our erstwhile consumption. And we were rocking it. Wanting to win it even more, I decided to stop buying clothes. Back in grad school when I needed to lose weight, I didn't pare down to, say, a few Cheetos per week; I banned them wholesale from my life. I needed this same rigor in order to stop buying clothes. If I'd laid out some wishy-washy ground rules like, "Oh, I'll buy only necessities," I would've come up with an excuse for why a black taffeta dress with a gold lace overlay (something I do, in fact, own) was a "necessity." Instead, I imposed an all-out ban on buying clothes that included socks, underwear, shoes, and accessories. Clothes, like makeup, were emotional purchases for me. They filled a void in my self-worth, shopping for them was a hobby, and I let my outward appearance define me. Not buying clothes was a way to experience contentment with what I already owned instead of constantly wishing for something better or newer. I'd been letting my stuff control me; now, it was time to turn that the other way around. I didn't know it then, but I wouldn't buy a scrap of clothing for another three years.

Completing the womanly beauty trifecta, I needed to do something about my hair. For the entire first year of our extreme frugality, I debated my hair. Pre-frugality, I'd been spending $120 four times a year at that chic salon and, can I be honest here? My hair looked fabulous. Really fabulous. But spending more on hair than we were spending on household supplies and utilities in a month *combined* seemed ludicrous. Plus, I was sincere in my effort to sever the tether I'd woven between my self-worth and my appearance. If I'd been able to stop wearing makeup and stop buying clothes, I should be able to do something about my hair. So I stopped getting it cut. That was a fine solution for about a year, but I now had the same hairstyle I'd had in fifth grade: waist-length and straight, which was cute in 1995. Now? I looked like I'd joined a cult that forbids hair cutting.

I priced out Supercuts and was about to book myself in for what I was certain would be a disaster-with-shears for $25 when Nate asked if I wanted him to cut it. I'd been cutting his hair for years now, although granted, it was a buzz cut, which I think a six-year-old could manage. It's sort of like mowing a lawn; you just go in straight lines with some curves around the ears and then you're done. Nate and I had grown closer during this year of intense frugality because, in order to save money, we often had to do stuff together, like cut hair, as opposed to hiring someone. We'd learned to depend on each other to an extent that's uncommon in our culture of wash-and-fold laundry pickup and meal delivery services. Given this, I wasn't surprised he offered to cut it, but I wasn't thrilled either. My desire to plunge further into frugality was strong because I had a reminder of why we were doing this every single weekday when I sat in my cubicle from 9 a.m. to 5 p.m. And so, we did what we always do before tackling a project we're nervous about the repercussions of (such as when we had to replumb our kitchen): we researched it on the Internet. I found a florid hairdresser on YouTube who had a sixty-minute-long (not exaggerating) video of how to cut long hair into layers. After fifteen minutes, I decided he was overcomplicating the situation and reasoned we could skip a few steps, which I hoped wasn't like when we put our IKEA dresser together and had a pile of screws left over and then realized we'd installed the drawers backward and had to take the whole thing apart again at 10 p.m.

I wrote out bullet points for Nate to follow and we went into the bathroom. I micromanaged the whole process, which Nate tolerated moderately well, and after about thirty minutes (a lot less commentary and flourishes than our YouTube guy, but a lot more "Hold still and stop telling me what to do!"), we had a haircut. An actually quite good-looking haircut with layers that framed my makeup-free face. I was rather stunned because the whole time I was planning to go to the salon afterward and pay for a bob cut.

The haircut performed by Nate wasn't quite the level of perfection of my $120 cut, but it was a darn nice facsimile that we'd gotten for free. I never went to a salon again. It brings a new level of intimacy to a marriage when your husband cuts your hair. Rather than this being a stressful, divisive experience, it gave us another opportunity to collaborate, to depend on each other, to weave our bond tighter, and to be partners in every sense. I grew up believing that cutting your own hair is something done only by 1) three-year-olds, 2) postbreakup women convinced they need bangs after consuming an entire bottle of Chablis, and 3) anyone in a cult (they really have PR issues around hair). I'd paid for haircuts every three months of my life without ever testing this theory for myself. We can brainwash ourselves into thinking we can't solve anything on our own without expensive interventions. Yet I find over and over and over again that when I actually audit this conventional wisdom, I uncover a flimsy veneer that's easily dismantled by a determined frugal person.

In the course of undoing my previously conventional, time-consuming, and expensive beauty routines, I came to realize that women are expected to look, dress, act, and even *think* a certain way. Despite being an avowed feminist married to a guy who took Advanced Theories in Feminist Thought with me our senior year of college, I'd hewed to mainstream expectations levied on women. I'd worn makeup and heels when I didn't want to, bought clothes I didn't need, and paid close to $500 a year for someone to clip my split ends. But that path never brought me fulfillment. All it did was enroll me in an endless carousel of consumerism that spun around and around, promising I'd reach perfection after the next turn, but instead pummelled me with prompts to buy more stuff. I'd internalized what society said was important, and made it important to me. I was learning that this pursuit of perfection I'd enslaved myself to from the age of fourteen was a hoax. It was designed to keep me buying things I didn't need and working a job I didn't care about, in order to slot myself into preconceived societal expectations. I was done with that.

I'd started out simply not wanting to spend money on makeup, clothes, and hair, and yes, I was now on track to save thousands every year in those categories. Much more profound, however, was the change this brought about in my thinking. I'd built confidence from the knowledge that I was OK on my own, bared as I was of makeup and stripped of new clothes and without expensive hair. I was still a valuable person. I was still smart and worthwhile. And I daresay, I now had more to say. All I did was stop doing things. I didn't go on a pilgrimage or have a near-death experience or get a makeover, I just gave up unnecessary activities of consumption. In doing so, I transformed how I felt about myself. I was no longer preoccupied with my appearance; I was preoccupied with changing myself, with evolving and maturing. I'd thought my maturation was finished in high school when I stepped onto this consumer carousel, but I now saw there was a world I could live in on my own terms. I was born again. Letting go of caring what other people thought enabled me to figure out what I really wanted out of life, not what society wanted out of my life. I came to understand that, in the end, the only person who truly cares how you live your life is you.

9

What Is Financial Independence Anyway?

It'd been over a year since Nate and I made the decision to abandon our conventional lives, and we were smack in the doldrums of our three-year plan: still working, still living in the city, but resolved that this wasn't our destiny. Our early months of extreme frugality were punctuated by the heady lust of novelty. We'd thrilled at each new dollar saved and frugal hack uncovered. But now, we'd reached what we considered our peak level of frugality with a savings rate that crested 82 percent some months, a percentage that didn't even include our 401(k) contributions or mortgage principal. There wasn't anything left to innovate with our savings; it was simply a matter of depositing money into our accounts every month and waiting for the totals to reach the number that would equal our financial independence.

The phrase "financial independence" is a bit problematic in its vagueness, and there are many different interpretations of what exactly it entails. I view financial independence as the point at which you no longer have to earn money in order to live. In other words, your assets are such that you can live off of them without the influx of a monthly paycheck. If you want to work you can, but you don't have to in order to pay your bills and feed your family. You are freed from the need to earn money; ergo, you are financially independent. This is what Nate and I were working toward. We wanted to have enough money saved up such that we could choose to work if we wanted to, but wouldn't have to work in order to survive. Nate and I determined that we'd be financially independent when a sustainable rate of withdrawal from our assets comfortably exceeded our conservative expense projections.

Once Nate and I were financially independent, our assets would comprise the following five elements:

1. 401(k)s. The first components were our traditional retirement accounts, which in our case were an employer-sponsored 401(k) and an employer-sponsored 403(b). Nate and I each contributed the IRS-specified maximum amount to our respective accounts each year, which at the time was $18,000 annually. You can determine the current maximum allowable contribution limit by checking the IRS website. Our employers also contributed a percentage to these accounts each year, called a "match," which is a benefit that's offered by some em-

ployers. If your employer offers a matching 401(k) or 403(b), start contributing to it today because those matching funds are *free money*. Contributions to these accounts are pretax and can't be accessed without penalties before age 59.5. I will note that there are exceptions to this rule, such as the Roth IRA conversion ladder; but in general, you shouldn't touch a 401(k) until you're 59.5. The reason Nate and I chose to contribute such large amounts to these accounts is twofold. First of all, our employers both offered a match, which means they deposited money into our accounts as a bonus for us contributing money into these accounts. Sounds like an impossible unicorn of free money, but it's real! If you're not sure what your company offers in terms of retirement plans, ask your HR department tomorrow. Or later today. Or right now. Seriously, put the book down and send them an email this instant. The reason to start contributing to a 401(k) or 403(b) at a young age is the power of compounding interest. The earlier you invest money in the market, the more money you'll make because the longer you'll be invested. Do not wait until you're older—it'll be too late to benefit from that compounding interest.

The second reason Nate and I were such avid 401(k) proponents is that contributions to 401(k)s are made pretax, which means these contributions lower your taxable income. This is a good thing because it means you pay less in taxes now. Yes, you do have to pay taxes when you withdraw this money at age 59.5 or older, but the linchpin is that your tax rate will likely be lower at that age, because you're likely to have stopped working. If you're not retired at 59.5, wait until you are before you begin making withdrawals from your 401(k). By doing this, you reduce your tax burden in your highest earning years and then you pay those taxes in your lowest earning years. Tax rates are calibrated off of your income, so this works in your favor. Another advantage? Many employers offer the ability to contribute to your 401(k) directly from your paycheck, so you never even see the money or have the chance to consider spending it. It's a great way to force/motivate yourself to save.

2. Investments in the form of low-fee index funds. This is where the bulk of my cash hangs out. Index funds are, in my opinion, the best way to invest because the fees are low, you can manage them yourself, and they often outperform actively managed funds. Index funds are also ideal because they're a heavily diversified way to invest, since you're invested across the entire market. But the real win with index funds is their absence of high fees, which are what you'll encounter with a portfolio manager and what will *cripple* your net worth in the long run.

The reason to invest in the market, as opposed to keeping all of your money in a checking or savings account, is that investing is how you build wealth. In order for your money to make money, a certain amount of risk must be undertaken. Historically, the stock market has generated a 7 percent average annual return. And yes, the market does go up and down because that's the very nature of the stock market. But the thing to remember is that history demonstrates that the market always eventually goes up. Even after the Great Recession, the market rebuilt itself. Not immediately, but over time. Successful investing entails the following: buying and holding diversified, low-fee stocks for decades, avoiding the temptation to time the market, not pulling money in and out of the market, and not following the market on a daily basis. Invest and hold (for years upon years) and, more likely than not, your money will make more money.

This is an oversimplification of investing, and there are other variables such a rebalancing and asset allocation, as well as decreasing your exposure to risk as you near traditional retirement age, but this is the basic gist. If you want to grow your wealth, you need to avail yourself of the stock market. Investing in low-fee index funds is as straightforward as any other facet of online banking, and you can set up an account online by yourself in minutes. You will need to select a brokerage that offers low-fee index funds, and then you will need to set up an account and transfer over some money to get started. In order to remove human error and the very human temptation to time the market, I simply invest money every month. Our account is set up to automatically invest a specified amount of money every month, so that we're constantly adding to our investments without concerning ourselves over what the market happens to be doing at a particular moment in time. As with 401(k)s, the best time to start investing was yesterday, and the second-best time is today.

3. Real estate. Our Cambridge home would become a revenue-generating rental property and we'd also own a homestead property, which would be our primary residence. We decided to hold on to our Cambridge home as a rental because it rents out at a rate that's comfortably cash flow positive, and it represents diversification in our otherwise index fund–heavy portfolio of assets. This property also provides us with a passive stream of income; in other words, we make money every month without needing to do anything for this money. We have a property manager for this rental, so we really don't do anything.

I will caution that this is a gross oversimplification of real estate investing, and I don't recommend diving into rentals without first doing thorough research. It's also very true that some markets are better for rentals than others. A great many factors go into whether or not a rental will be successful. I think it's telling that, despite a capacity to own more rental properties, Nate and I choose to stick with just this one. In many cases, there's a lot of risk and volatility involved with serving as a landlord, although it's also true that the return can be much greater than what one would experience in the stock market. All that is to say, it's another avenue for investing and generating passive income, but one that should be exhaustively researched.

4. A donor advised fund. Nate and I have a donor advised fund (DAF), which is a tax-advantaged vehicle through which we contribute to charities every year. DAFs allow donors to take a tax deduction for the full amount of their contribution to their fund in the calendar year that the contribution was made. In light of this, it's wise to start a DAF, and to deposit a significant amount of money into it during a high tax year for your family, as it reduces your taxable income for that year.

Then, donors allocate grants to nonprofits of their choice at any time they wish. DAFs are invested in the stock market, which means they grow tax-free, thus augmenting your overall base of philanthropic support. Thanks to this, DAFs are a wonderful way to ensure that Nate and I will be able to support charities for decades to come while avoiding capital gains taxes. I firmly believe that Nate and I are exceedingly fortunate and the beneficiaries of a great deal of privilege; hence, it's important to us that we give back. Supporting charities is an element of our financial plan that we wanted to enshrine in a formalized way. A DAF can be an excellent vehicle for strategically planning out your philanthropy for a lifetime.

5. Cash. Finally, we maintain around four months' to a year's worth of living expenses in cash, held in a good old-fashioned checking account. It's crucial to have some of your assets in cash (in a savings or checking account), as this serves as your emergency fund. If something catastrophic happens, you want to have sufficient cash on hand to handle the crisis without going into debt. For example, say you lose your job tomorrow and your car conveniently breaks down at the same time. You need enough money in your bank account to cover all of your living expenses (rent/mortgage, groceries, medicine, etc.) while you job search, *and* you need enough money to pay to fix your car so that you can drive to job interviews. Insert any other health crisis/urgent home repair/change in employment/family situation as an example of why you need an emergency fund.

If you're just starting out on your financial independence journey, one of the very first steps is to build up an emergency fund of cash. There's no substitute for this, and there's no way around it—you need to have readily available cash to serve as your buffer against calamity. A car, a house (even one that's paid off), or a set of expensive china does not count as emergency funds. Neither do stocks. Neither does real estate. In order to be financially sound, you must have at least three to six months' worth of living expenses saved up in a savings or checking account.

While this is the portfolio of assets that Nate and I have, your portfolio might be quite different, which is totally fine. There's no one right way to achieve financial stability and, eventually, financial independence. Here is a step-by-step plan that can serve as your guide for getting started:

1. Determine your goals. What do you want out of life? Where do you want to be in five years, ten years, forty years? In what ways are your finances helping or hindering your progress toward these goals?
2. Pay off any high-interest debt as quickly as possible (note: a fixed, low-interest rate mortgage is not included in this category). Debt is a drain on your long-term net worth and the financial equivalent of a ball and chain around your ankle. If you have high-interest debt you probably know all too well how expensive it can be.

Do yourself a favor, pay it down and don't go into debt again.

3. Building an emergency fund is absolutely crucial, as discussed above.

4. Contribute to some form of traditional retirement account, such as a 401(k) or 403(b), *especially* if your employer offers a matching contribution.

5. Create diversity in your assets, as we did with our real estate and stock market investments.

6. Grow your wealth, which in my case is through low-fee index funds and our rental property.

7. Embrace frugality in order to achieve all of these objectives more quickly and more sustainably.

If you can't save enough, even with a regimen of true extreme frugality, then you probably need to look for ways to earn more, either through finding a new job or adding on a second job or side hustle.

There are a number of different formulas that people use to determine how much money they'll need in order to reach financial independence, but at the most basic level, it's a question of how much money you need to live on every year. In light of that, there are actually only three variables in the financial independence equation: income, expenses, and time. The less you spend, the more you save, the faster you save it, and the less money you need overall. Considered in this context, frugality is a compounding proposition and one of the fastest ways to reach financial independence. A high salary alone is meaningless if you don't save any of it. The more distance you can put between your earnings and your expenses, the faster you'll reach any financial goal you set. While there are other factors that also must be considered, such as your personal tolerance for risk, dependents, and health care, a very basic definition of financial independence is as follows: when a sustainable level of withdrawals from your assets is more than your ongoing expenses.

Well that all sounds as good as a box of cupcakes. But the crucial third variable in achieving financial independence—time—became a sharp thorn stuck inside my left sock as we rounded our first year of goal pursuit. I need to be active, proactive, and busy. Waiting is not high on my list of preferred activities. My kindergarten report card said that I "demonstrated impatience." Mrs. Baumgartner was spot-on.

When Nate drives and I'm in the passenger seat, I clip my fingernails or work on my computer or write out a grocery list. Wasted time is anathema to me. Knowing I had to slog through another two years in a job I'd lost passion for, and a city I didn't want to live in, and a life I was done with, weighed me down. As I walked into work one morning, I felt like the walls in the hallway leading to my cubicle were narrowing. Still wearing my winter coat, which I'd found in a trash pile and then washed at a laundromat, I was overheated and already pressed down by the day, which had barely begun. My days felt like a Styrofoam of emotion: devoid of color and flavor, imprinted with the day that'd come before, promising me I'd be left disappointed. I longed for something vibrant to jolt me into consciousness.

In the past when Nate and I were ready for a change, we acted on it in a matter of months, if not weeks. But this plan, this unconventional idea to quit our jobs and start a homestead in Vermont, necessitated we wait for *years*. We could've packed our bags and moved immediately, but that would've entailed far less certainty, something in gross contradiction with our cautious, deliberative personalities. Nate and I are not spontaneous. Or reckless. Even though I knew we were taking the strategic route, one that would ensure we wouldn't end up penniless and living in a tent in the middle of someone's field, I hated that I was wishing my time away. I wanted the years to elapse so that we could get to our dream. I wasn't living, I was marking off days. It wasn't the frugality that bothered me; it was the waiting. It never crossed my mind to give up on our aspirations, even though going to work every day felt like wearing shoes that were too tight. For one thing, I was confident we were right about not wanting to spend the rest of our adult lives confined to offices, with no agency over our daily schedules. In fact, going to work every day served to further cement my conviction that this was the right choice for us. Perhaps even more crucially, we were actually enjoying the process of extreme frugality. Like, a lot.

10

Turns Out, Frugality Is About More Than Money. Much More.

The kitchen in our Cambridge home had this bulky, floor-to-ceiling cabinet that bisected the breakfast nook and demoted our otherwise respectable kitchen to a dim galley. Covered in shiny oak veneer, it was the unwanted hippopotamus of kitchen cabinets. Infected with the fever of new(ish) homeowners on a beautification kick and drunk with dreams of DIY, we decided to rip it out. Nate, thrilled with an excuse to use his Sawzall, dismantled the monstrosity. Of course it was only after he'd spent four hours hacking and ripping that we discovered there was no flooring underneath this particular cabinet. It'd been inserted atop '50s-era floral linoleum that was at least two floor choices previous to the current wood. That might not sound too bad, but there was also no wall behind the cabinet. We were now staring at two square feet of yellowed, floral vinyl and a floor-to-ceiling absence of drywall. Nate asked if it was too noticeable. Since this un-wall and un-floor faced the front door, the staircase, our bedroom, the kitchen, and the living room, I said it wasn't if you spent all of your time inside the bathroom.

Since keeping this Cambridge home as a rental property after we made our move to the woods was a key aspect of our financial independence plan, we decided to tackle cosmetic renovations in order to boost the home's appeal (and hopefully, the rental price). First up were the kitchen cabinets, all of which were '90s-era holdovers reeking of golden oak ugliness. Rather than rip them all out, a judicious call made after the lessons learned from hippo cabinet, we decided to paint them white. I called around to a few professional cabinet painters (that's a thing, as it turns out) and they returned quotes starting at $2,000 and escalating from there. For a small kitchen! With not that many cabinets! Especially with the hippo cabinet gone! And so, as would happen many times in the years to come, Nate and I elected to do the project ourselves. Neither of us had ever done such a thing before, but we were determined to figure it out. You can do just about anything yourself with the aid of the Internet, short of medical, dental, or veterinary surgery, none of which I recommend DIY-ing.

For three weekends in a row, Nate and I disassembled, sanded, stripped, painted white, and then reassembled our kitchen. I employed approximately 658 plastic sandwich bags to sort and label the millions of pieces of hardware that are apparently necessary for keeping cabinet doors attached. After reassembling everything using my Type A numbered plastic baggie system, the kitchen looked fabulous! At the very least, it looked white! It wasn't perfect—there are some things I'd do differently next time, such as buy an electric sander instead of sanding every inch by hand—but we were delighted. After this husband-wife DIY adventure, we realized we were actually happier with the end result than we would've been if we'd hired someone. In addition to spending only $183.45 (versus the $2,000), we were the beneficiaries of what researchers call the "IKEA effect." It's proven that people experience greater satisfaction with projects they do themselves, even if the result is subpar, than with projects they pay other people to do. When we pay for a service, we expect a level of perfection that's unattainable. But when we do it ourselves, we know the effort and hard work that went into the process, which leads to a higher degree of contentment with the finished product. Through our now-white kitchen cabinets, the first nonmonetary benefit of frugality was revealed to me.

Back in March 2014, on day one of this journey, I'd seen frugality as the necessary means to our end. What I hadn't anticipated was that it would become an end in and of itself. After a solid year of spending money only on the fundamentals of life, the very *basest* items to get us by (food, our mortgage, gas for the car, electricity, an Internet connection, toilet paper, and the like), Nate and I felt like we'd unlocked a map that led us out of our previous maze of mindless consumption, which hadn't suited us.

We wondered if anyone else had discovered the liberation of not spending money, of not being beholden to anyone but yourself. I was like somebody's great-aunt who discovered the curative powers of kombucha and will not shut up about it. I solved the temptation to evangelize by never talking about frugality with anyone in real life. I poured my zeal into Frugalwoods, since I figured it was an elective audience, not just the person who unwittingly unfurled their mat next to me in yoga. From outward appearances, I lived a supremely conventional life. I was married, I had a job, I owned a house, I bathed daily, I had a dog that I could be seen walking around the neighborhood. But on the inside? I was a double agent who'd figured out that our consumer culture had co-opted our need for community, for safety, and for love, and packaged it up as something to be bought. Since Nate and I weren't sharing our plans with our friends or coworkers just yet, I felt as though no one knew or understood me. Frugality didn't just become part of our lives; it transformed our lives and became our worldview, our philosophy, and very nearly a religion. We'd started out with an urgency around saving money, but it evolved to be about much more than that. It became a wholesale lifestyle transformation.

Nate and I began to uncover far-reaching advantages to frugality that outstripped the mechanics of spending less cash and growing our net worth. The satisfaction we derived from painting our own kitchen cabinets was the first tertiary benefit we discovered, and the second was close behind: doing this project together brought us closer in our marriage. For the first time since a group paper for our International Elections course in college, Nate and I were teammates on projects with tangible results. Our modern culture has largely done away with the idea that a marriage—or a civil union or a partnership—is a working relationship, and instead touts the money-focused solution of "Don't fight, hire out!" The answer to our hectic, frenzied, compulsive lives isn't to simplify, it's to pay other people to do stuff for us so that we can pile ever more on our already gluttonous to-do plates. This is exactly the routine Nate and I fell into when we lived in DC, and all it served to do was drive us apart. In fact, it very nearly wrecked the close-knit intimacy we'd created during our uncomplicated early days of marriage in that basement apartment. We were able to claw back our relationship through the teamwork of hiking, but the communication and problem-solving that's required for frugal insourcing is by far one of the most profound experiences we've had in our marriage. In addition to the expense of hiring out, doing so pulled us away from sharing a unified goal. When we weren't teammates, Nate and I weren't on the same page financially or in terms of what we wanted out of life. And it's very hard to craft a satisfying life with another person when you're not in agreement over how to spend your two most precious resources: your time and your money.

I chose to spend my life with Nate for a reason. I trusted him, I thought he was smart, and we worked well together, so it only made sense to consider him my partner in every sense. Collaborating on repainting our kitchen cabinets was the first of many projects that allowed me to see his skills shine, and brought a new level of respect to our relationship. We'd compliment each other on a job well done, we'd help each other on complex elements of a project, and I noticed that we started saying "please" and "thank you" to each other in the course of our daily routine. I began to recognize all the work that Nate put into our household and he did the same for me. Gratitude and respect began to infuse our interactions. It's easy to discount your partner's contributions until you're standing side by side in the kitchen, watching them chop vegetables for forty-five minutes just to cook you up a stir-fry you love for dinner.

As we expanded our repertoire of frugal insourcing, we also learned new skills we'd be able to use long into the future. When you do something yourself, you permanently reduce your dependency on outside sources and permanently increase your own aptitudes. It's very much a "teaching a person to fish" proposition. From that one kitchen project, we were empowered to teach ourselves how to do everything from plumbing to haircuts. And we did. I also want to point out that insourcing within a partnership doesn't mean that one partner now has nine billion more chores to do. It means that both members of the partnership vote on an equitable division of labor, and execute their respective tasks. In my experience, frugal insourcing leads to a more egalitarian partnership devoid of traditional gender roles and reliant instead upon a system of routines and an agreed-upon divvying up of tasks. We never debate who will cook, because that's exclusively in Nate's wheelhouse, and we never argue over who will clean, because that's my job. Our division of household chores is so deeply ingrained that I don't even make my own coffee in the mornings, and I'm pretty sure Nate doesn't know how to operate our washing machine. We're each experts in our chosen domestic fields and, indeed, Nate's already fantastic cooking improves year after year, and my housecleaning gets faster every time I do it. I find that by repeatedly performing the same chores, we've become more proficient and more efficient in our duties.

As Nate and I were rescuing a perfectly good lamp and dresser from a roadside pile of trash one Saturday morning, I had an epiphany: frugality is excellent for the environment. Under the auspices of frugality, Nate and I were consuming less and reusing more. We drastically reduced the amount of stuff we bought, and when we did buy something, we almost always got it secondhand. By diverting used items from the waste stream, we were simultaneously decreasing the carbon footprint inherent to producing new materials and preventing usable goods from clogging landfills. Nearly every frugal strategy doubles as a boon for the environment. I'm of the belief that you can't buy your way to green because consumption, by its very action, usually has a negative impact on the environment. Frugality, conversely, incorporates environmentalism into your lifestyle. It's also true that the less we consume, the more we respect and care for the things we already own. Instead of viewing our material possessions as disposable items marching along the chain of consumption, Nate and I started to see our stuff as long-term residents of our home. Nate patched holes in his pants, I refinished old furniture, and we didn't throw out anything except for actual trash. Our convenience culture tries to indoctrinate an unending, unquenchable thirst for more. For newer. For better. For bigger. But most of all, for more. Nate and I were now outsiders in this arms race of possessions. We didn't care if people judged our car as junky (which, at nineteen years old and with over 200,000 miles, it was), or our clothes as dated, because we knew that once you enroll in the buying-leads-to-fulfillment mentality, there's no end to how much you'll have to purchase. As soon as you update your phone and refurbish your bathroom and get this season's hottest boots, trends will change. You'll find yourself with a phone that lacks a hologram, a bathroom with gold finishes when silver is now in vogue, and you'll wonder why you ever thought orange patent-leather boots were a good idea. Nate and I decided to just say no. We finally acknowledged that we had enough. Enough clothing, enough throw pillows, enough dinner plates. This acknowledgement also imbued me with a mind-set of giving. Instead of tossing out old stuff, I gave it away to friends, to thrift stores, and to my Buy Nothing group. I realized that precious few things are actually trash.

In our drive to spend less money, I discovered a multitude of other ways that we could limit our consumption. I began to hang more of our laundry up on racks to dry, instead of tossing it into our energy-gulping dryer. I now considered how long my showers were, how often I drove our car, how high we turned up our heat, and what kind of lightbulbs we used. Frugality made me conscious of everything we bought, consumed, threw out, needed, and didn't need. Before bringing anything into our house, I questioned if I wanted to assume the responsibility of storing it, cleaning it, and eventually, finding a new home for it. It was a comprehensive revolution of how I interact with resources. Consumerism, on the other hand, removes those realities. It encourages us to discard anything we're bored with, buy more, and gobble as many resources as we can possibly swallow.

Consumerism made me into an insatiable, grabbing taker, whereas frugality transformed me into a mindful, grateful giver. Once I turned on this mind-set of spending less, and as a consequence using fewer natural resources, I was amazed at all the areas where I could simultaneously conserve money and fossil fuels. This unanticipated benefit of upping our environmentalism and decreasing our carbon footprint redoubled my commitment to lifelong frugality. My frugality became about something broader and more momentous than simply the money I could save in my bank account. It was about my impact on our earth. It was about what I could do with my time and how I could interact with the world.

The concept that we had enough also began to influence the way we ate. I abolished food waste from our kitchen. Nate made conscious decisions in the grocery store to buy only precisely what he planned to cook that week, and then we committed ourselves to eating that food in its entirety and not giving in to the temptation of Thai takeout. This benefited us because we spent a lot less on food and ate more healthfully, but perhaps more crucially, it benefited the environment by producing less landfill-bound garbage. Discarded food is one of the most significant components of landfills and is a major methane producer, which is a greenhouse gas that contributes to climate change. Food is but one usable product we humans relegate to landfills. Carelessly tossed clothing, furniture, and electronics also populate our planet's piles of refuse. By embracing frugality, Nate and I became aware of the role that needless waste plays in our lives and of the ways we could fight back against it.

I also uncovered a tipping point that exists wherein an inanimate object takes on a level of importance exceeding its intended function. Kids do this with stuffed animals; adults do this with everything from furniture to shoes. I started considering all of my purchases through this lens. Did I *need* a new coat in order to keep warm? Or did I *want* a new coat in order to look cute? Usually the latter. Cars are the most insidious example because our culture equates car ownership with status, a ridiculous metric for a machine whose intended function is to safely convey you from point A to point B. Nate and I saw our nineteen-year-old minivan for what it was: a car that drove. As a status or beauty symbol? Not so much. But we didn't need a new car to validate our self-worth. We didn't feel a compulsion to announce our material success to the person driving behind us. In addition to no longer caring what others thought about us, we let go of the need to prove ourselves through external objects because we thought that wasn't the way to achieve deep, lasting contentment. We weren't at that level of contentment yet, as we were still experiencing the slog of working toward our goal. But since rampant consumerism had failed to make us happy, I was really hoping that avoiding it would do the trick. If I were to buy a new car, I'd experience a hedonic jolt of dopamine when I first made the purchase and then, gradually, the newness would wear off, the rush of adrenaline would die down, and I'd be casting around for my next hit of consumerism to start the cycle all over again.

Something I learned on my journey to consume less is that material possessions should not be forced or expected to serve as stand-ins for human emotions. Things do not bring me fulfillment. Sure, they might be nice to have, but we shouldn't expect everything we own to bring us some deep, Kondo-esque sense of "joy." Our consumer culture erects shrines to stuff and encourages us to measure our worth by what we can buy. There's even an entire industry devoted to helping us organize and store all of the excess stuff we've bought that we don't have the time and space to use, let alone savor. Through frugality, I came to understand that it's entirely reasonable, and much cheaper, to own things that simply serve their intended function. Because when we tell ourselves that our stuff needs to bring us *joy*, we begin to justify spending money on everything that we think might *possibly* achieve that desire for us, rather than working to find joy from within. Things are not people, things do not fulfill us, and expecting them to serve that function will only lead to a string of expensive disappointments.

Around this time, I also began to see the irony inherent to the classic American pastime of going to the gym. Think about it: we pay other people to clean our houses, wash our cars, walk our dogs, prepare our meals, do our shopping, mow our lawns, and watch our children, so that we can pay even more money to go inside a building to run and lift on machines that simulate doing those chores. Nate rode his bike to work every single day, even through Boston winters, which was a triple boon: it saved money, it was good for the environment, and it provided him with daily exercise. The more we frugalized, the more we understood the far-reaching, positive repercussions of this lifestyle. Nate and I were undoing decades of training we'd received to be obedient capitalists. We were harkening to an earlier era, when people were self-reliant and didn't look for meaning on store shelves.

These revelations also led me to realize that paying money is the laziest, least creative way to solve a problem or reach a desired end. There's no innovation in slapping down a credit card. At first, this was challenging for me. For example: how do I find someone to watch our dog for free instead of paying to board her at a kennel? Then it dawned on me that this was an opportunity to build community. I reached out to fellow dog-owning friends. We worked out an informal dog-sitting swap that didn't entail money changing hands. We were happier, the dogs were happier, and we reaped the tertiary benefit of creating a community, another artifact we were resurrecting from our ancestors that'd been all but stamped out by commercialism. A frugal life is a creative life and one that's devoid of clutter, both physical and mental, and absent any boredom.

In my quest to save money, I always had a project to work on, a solution to innovate, or a hack to uncover.

Perhaps most significant during this year of revelations was our recognition that frugality gave us options. Too often, the arc of our lives and the very substance of what we do day after day is dictated to us by our jobs, our debt, and our stuff. Frugality enabled Nate and me to wrest back control. When you're not reliant on the salary from a job, and you're not embattled by debt, and you're not controlled by your things, your options for how to use your time and how to impact your world are suddenly quite open. Frederick Buechner once said, "Your vocation in life is where your greatest joy meets the world's greatest need." I firmly believe frugality can enable you to discern, and follow, your vocation because it removes the necessity of choosing work based primarily on remuneration. You could quit your job and travel the world, you could explore your passion for woodworking, you could volunteer full time at an animal shelter. None of these paths are closed to any of us, save the fact that we've usually put ourselves in a financial position that makes these pursuits impossible. It's not about how much you like or dislike your job, it's about how dependent upon it you are for your paycheck. Frugality is the difference between a job loss or a health issue or a new roof being a crisis or merely an inconvenience. Frugality constructs a buffer between you and the unforeseen, yet entirely predictable, disasters of life. By saving more than you need, and by not living paycheck to paycheck, you grant yourself the security of knowing that you can weather a crisis without going into debt. Frugality frees you from the day-to-day anguish of managing a rigid budget. When you operate with the worldview that there's very little you need to buy, you no longer need to count pennies or worry if there's enough money in your account. You're set.

Reflecting on this idea, here's a question: Why can't you quit your job? The only right answer is, "because I love my job and I don't want to quit." Anything other than that means you're serving masters not in alignment with your truest wishes. Strip away all of the spending that doesn't strike at the heart of your long-term goals, and you'll have the life you actually want to live. Don't allow your spending to prevent you from doing what you want; instead, allow frugality to sculpt the life you crave.

11

Fighting Back Against the Baby-Industrial Complex

"Does that look like a blue line to you?" I asked Nate as we huddled in the bathroom together first thing in the morning, shining a flashlight on a four-inch-long plastic stick. Neither of us could tell, at least not definitively enough for what this particular blue line portended, so we took a 6:15 a.m. walk the six blocks to the dollar store to buy more tests. I took tests number three and four and by test number five, we were pretty sure there *was* a blue line, but I wondered why the manufacturers didn't make it a "YOU ARE PREGNANT" sign in flashing neon. This whole blue line thing just wasn't very convincing. So I called my doctor, who said I could come in for a blood test if I really wanted to, but that it wouldn't tell us anything more than the blue line had. True, I thought, but you can interpret my blood with state-of-the-art lab equipment and a person who had to go to school for this, not me in a bathroom with a flashlight, doubting my eyesight and the veracity of a piece of plastic that cost $3.99.

My desperation must've been obvious to the doctor, that or the fact that I was plastered with sweat on account of jogging the twelve blocks to her office. So they called me back with the results that evening, just as some friends walked through our front door for a dinner party. I welcomed our friends with a delusional grin, then pulled Nate into our coat closet to tell him it was definitely a blue line. I still had trouble believing it, so I started googling around for how accurate a blood test is at confirming pregnancy. It wasn't until after our first ultrasound when we saw a tiny blob that the technician assured us (repeatedly) was a baby that I fully accepted we were going to have a child.

Fifteen months before this blue line appeared, Nate and I opened up our shared calendar and decided that the optimal time to birth our first child would be precisely November 15, 2014. This would be right after Nate's busy season at work, so he'd be able to stay home with me and the baby until after the new year. Plus, I'd have been in my job for the requisite time to accrue maternity leave. Counting back forty weeks, we calculated that we should start trying on Monday, February 3, 2014. In case you're wondering, attempting to plan a child's exact birthdate exemplifies my need for control. Starting on Monday, February 3, 2014, Nate and I tracked ovulation, marked the calendar, counted days, and took tests. And for thirteen months, nothing happened. Not even a nebulous blue line.

On month twelve of trying to conceive, we found ourselves in the waiting room of a fertility specialist who was adjacent to an obstetrician's office. Nate and I sat there, palms sweating, reading pamphlets titled "IVF: Not as Painful as You Think" while glowing, globular, pregnant women sailed past on their way to ultrasounds and a lifetime of childbearing bliss. Some of them even had older children with them. The nerve. I couldn't understand why we weren't getting pregnant. Had the fertility gods not read the statistics? That children do better with two parents? That children do better in a home that's financially secure? That children do better when mothers have advanced degrees? I mean, please! I was eating kale daily, going to yoga thrice weekly, and considering both acupuncture and something called the Maya fertility massage. I was booked in for a set of increasingly invasive and ominously named tests and waiting the requisite month to get on the schedule to start intrauterine insemination (IUI).

It was while waiting for our appointed IUI start date that this blue line appeared. My first thought was all the wine I'd drunk that week. I'd abstained almost entirely for those thirteen months of trying, but I'd given up the charade of assuming pregnancy that month because I couldn't take the disappointment yet again. I called the fertility specialist to cancel our IUI appointment and starting crying on the phone. I just couldn't believe it had happened. Through our very brief, very painless interaction with infertility, Nate and I found something we couldn't control. Something we couldn't pop into a spreadsheet or create an efficiency for. I know that many couples endure years of painful, challenging circumstances around trying to conceive and I'm keenly aware that our experience was nothing by comparison. With the wisdom and benevolence of retrospect—plus the fact that I like to make myself look good—I can say that it was a humbling experience that taught me the value of patience. But honestly, at the time I was just angry. I'd always assumed I'd be able to have biological children, that this rite of womanhood would come easily to me. I was in excellent physical condition, I ate all kinds of green things, and I was in a mature relationship. I wasn't prepared for the whims of fertility and the utter lack of control I had over my own body. After six months, and then ten months, and then finally a year, we made contingency plans: we could adopt, or have a pack of dogs, or make peace with the idea of childlessness. So this blue line, this apparent baby, felt like eating pizza followed by ice cream cake followed by a release of balloons with white doves cooing at my feet while a rainbow burst across the sky and a marching band went past carrying a banner proclaiming: "YOU are pregnant!" It was almost too much happiness for one person's body to contain, so I wondered if boundless joy could negatively impact a fetus (verdict: it does not appear so).

The very next morning I started worrying about the baby surviving the precarious first trimester. It's nearly impossible for me to rest in happiness because my brain picks away until it finds something fresh to worry over. I'd compulsively read every book on pregnancy that the Cambridge Public Library had in stock (some books twice, and I had to pay a late fine on another) so I was all too aware of the chances for miscarriage. Despite this excessive anxiety, I breezed through the first trimester and learned the first two universal parenting lessons: 1) you are not in control, and 2) there is *always* something to worry about where your children are concerned.

The third "truth" I kept hearing is that children are always, and without exception, expensive. I don't even know how this yarn wended its way into my brain, but it's a pervasive trope in our culture and one that's lobbed at every expectant parent by advertisers, baby books, obstetricians, and of course fellow parents. In addition to the excitement I felt over, you know, *having* a baby, a close second was the excitement Nate and I had for our plans to entirely upend this hackneyed conventional wisdom. Yes, having a child is more expensive than not having a child, but it doesn't have to cost anywhere near the egregious sums I see headlining clickbait scare-tactic articles designed to send already apprehensive pregnant women—neurotically scanning the Internet while inhaling ice cream (speaking for myself here . . .)—into near panic attacks.

By the time we finally got pregnant in March 2015, Nate

and I had figured out how to apply extreme frugality to every aspect of our lives. We reasoned parenthood shouldn't be any different. Once you've ingrained the mind-set of frugality and reaped the multitude of benefits the lifestyle offers, it's actually more difficult to spend money than not. There's an assumption that parenting is somehow impossible to square with frugality, but let me ruin the rest of the book and divest you of this notion right now: it's not. There's a stigma associated with used baby things and yes, babies are expensive if you care what other people think about your diaper bag and burp cloths. Nate and I learned that the stuff of babies, the rockers, bouncers, and changing tables, was all around us, in the attics and basements of everyone we knew with kids slightly too old to sleep in a crib any longer. Before we even got pregnant, my friend at work mentioned that she needed to transition her youngest son into a big boy bed and that she didn't know what to do with his crib and changing table, since she couldn't sell the crib, an old drop-side model, on Craigslist. She figured she'd have to throw it out. My frugal antenna went up, way up, and I asked her if I could have it. Nate and I took the minivan over to her house one Sunday and spent the afternoon disassembling the crib and changing table and squeezing them into the back of the van. We'd long since taken all the rear seats out of the minivan, rendering it a sort of pick-up truck with a roof, because either we or our friends were forever hauling furniture or two-by-fours or, in one memorable instance while dog sitting, three grey-hounds.

As Nate worked to take apart the crib, my friend and her husband, thrilled we were carting away this old stuff, asked if we wanted any other baby things. She pulled out a high chair, car seat, changing pads, clothes, crib sheets, toys, books; a gold mine of hand-me-downs. She was surprised we wanted all this old stuff, but delighted to unload it. Nate and I stored this stash in our upstairs guest room (where I wouldn't see it and weep during my un-pregnancy) for al-most a year and a half before our daughter was born. Hous-ing this stuff for so long was worth it to us for what turned out to be a nursery we spent all of $20 on. Baby things are like Christmas trees: when it's in season, you really want it, but once that season is over, you want it out of your house like yesterday. Once I was pregnant, I put out the word to friends, neighbors, coworkers (anyone I knew with kids) that I'd happily take their hand-me-downs. Most of them were initially surprised that I wanted used things since, as an upper-middle-class urban couple expecting their first precious child, it was assumed we'd want to buy brand-new, top-of-the-line baby gear. After people heard I'd take their castoffs, a mother lode of baby goods came pouring in. I also joined my local Buy Nothing group, which was a bastion of baby and kid stuff. I started cleaning out our basement and gave away wedding gifts we'd never opened, picture frames, throw pillows, and anything else we didn't need in exchange for bibs, clothes, blankets, books, toys, a stroller, swaddles, a bassinet, and more. All well used and all completely free.

The insidious thing about new baby paraphernalia is that manufacturers and marketers know they're dealing with a vulnerable, susceptible demographic: expectant parents. If there's a more anxiety-provoking time than being pregnant with your first child, I'd like to hear about it. Because you are now weighted with the gravity of knowing you're going to be responsible for another person, a life you've created. After all, *don't you want what's best for your child?* What's safest? What's most likely to ensure their spot in Harvard's class of 2037?! Any special occasion or life event is an advertiser's dream, and weddings, graduations, and funerals are all ripe for cowing participants into spending way more than they can afford because, as the ads taunt: "you deserve it" and "everyone else is doing it" and "don't you want to honor your loved ones?" The golden goose of all is the baby-industrial complex. The pressure is so compelling that if Nate and I weren't already secure, confident, and well-practiced in our frugality, I would've been sucked right into the fray. As it was, I was firmly off the consumer carousel and suspicious of claims that used baby stuff was gross or unsafe. These ads play on our basest fears that we won't be able to provide for our children, that they'll get sick, that they'll be unhappy. But buying stuff doesn't mitigate any of those concerns. If anything, it enhances them, since by buying tons of stuff, we'll have less money to deal with potentially serious issues, such as an unexpected health crisis.

There are very real safety considerations with baby goods, so I'm not recommending that anyone go all 1820s on their child and forgo modern conventions like sleep sacks and car seats. Merely that you use your brain. I know my brain took a hiatus during pregnancy, but bear with me. Nate and I accepted a hand-me-down car seat, an action that's cited as the ultimate parenting sin; however, we took that car seat from a trusted friend who told us the seat hadn't ever been in an accident. We then researched the serial number and manufacturer, and determined the seat wasn't expired and that there were no safety recalls or innovations. In other words, it was a perfectly fine free car seat. Same story for our high chair, which did in fact have a safety recall so we ordered the parts to fix it from the manufacturer, which, by the way, were free. And as for that drop-side crib? My friend had already installed the conversion kit that turned it into a safe, fixed-side crib. I probably wouldn't use a twenty-year-old car seat, but a two-year-old seat? Absolutely. We also played the long game in assembling our nursery, which is the heart of successful hand-me-downing. You can't expect to find everything you need in a day, a week, or even a month. It takes time to curate an entirely secondhand home, but as someone who has done it, I can tell you it's altogether possible.

Plus, the thrill of the hunt is unparalleled. When you

walk into a store and buy everything you could possibly need, you deprive yourself of the unadulterated providence of happening upon just the ExerSaucer you need sitting for free on the side of the road. There's no rush quite like it. My dear friend Torrey asked if she could host a baby shower for us and I was conflicted by her offer. On one hand, it was an incredibly sweet gesture and a shower would be a lot of fun. But on the other hand, I didn't want to condemn my friends to buying brand-new stuff for me when I knew I could find the things I needed for free or cheap on the used market. It felt unfair and out of alignment with my frugal ethos. And so I asked Torrey if she would instead be willing to keep our dog for us when we went to the hospital to have our baby. She very kindly agreed. Torrey explained that she wanted to do something to support us during this time and if dog sitting was what we needed, then she would do it. Forgoing a registry and baby shower might be unconventional, but it worked for me and it made me feel like I was able to keep true to my anticonsumer goals. Plus, we genuinely needed a dog sitter and were grateful to be able to take Torrey up on her generosity.

Frugality also eliminates the paralysis by analysis that's endemic to buying new. If we'd decided to buy everything new, hours of our lives (and a fair bit of sanity) would've been lost to comparing the merits of a City Mini versus a Snap-N-Go and an Ergo versus a Snugli. By taking whatever came our way for free, the time and stress endemic to making these choices was eliminated. More choices do not lead to more happiness. In fact, research has proven the exact opposite. When we're overwhelmed with the sixty-seven different styles of baby onesies, we're not going to be satisfied with our choice; no matter what, we'll wonder if we chose the wrong one. We'll second-guess our decision and compulsively read reviews to see if we're vindicated in our selection. Conversely, I was thrilled with any and all free baby onesies because I didn't have to labor over selecting them. Didn't hurt that I didn't pay for them either. We're led to believe that having the ability to select between multiple options is a boon, but in reality, any time we choose stuff over our circumstances, we're losing. The real freedom of choice is to turn our backs on consumption. You're not exerting your free will in spending money, you're turning your free will over to someone else. Choice is the ultimate freedom we have, yet so many of us put choice of material possessions ahead of choice over how we spend our lives.

In addition to decreasing our happiness level, endless choices also ratchet up our spending. If the $300 stroller is good, then the $375 model must be better . . . and we're now reading through the 276 customer reviews and it looks like people actually prefer the $425 model, which comes with a cup holder . . . open a few more tabs and it seems that there was an improvement made at the $450 level and so maybe that would be best . . . although actually, the $556 model is the one with five stars . . . and on it goes. Our unfettered access to massive data sets, scrolling customer reviews, and online forums has created an unrealistic expectation of exhaustive research before buying a single solitary thing. Purchasing a bib turns into a hair-tearing, nightmarish landscape of horror stories about babies smeared with irrevocably staining beet juice! (Side note: beets really do stain babies something awful.)

Is my high chair the best, most perfect, highest rated high chair ever designed for babies? Probably not. But it works mighty fine, and I wasted none of this time and mental energy. I just picked it up for free one afternoon from Nate's colleague, whose kids had outgrown it. And I actually like this high chair quite a bit, as it's cute, it's functional, and it cleans up well. I'd wager I appreciate it all the more because of the embodied time, stress, and cost that it *doesn't* represent. Plus, what's new today will probably be recalled or changed or otherwise modified for the next buying season to ensure we continue worshipping at the altar of eternal consumption.

I didn't suspend my own personal clothes-buying ban during pregnancy either. I figured if I could find so many baby things secondhand, surely I could source hand-me-down maternity clothes too. And I did. Everything from nursing tank tops to maternity cocktail dresses came my way for free as hand-me-downs. Maternity clothes that you wear only for a few months tops? Total rip-off. My collection of hand-me-downs weren't all perfect, weren't all my style, weren't all my size, and some were downright shabby, but they *were* all free and they all worked just fine. I managed to look professional every day at my job (plus requisite work cocktail parties), participate in several conferences, go to a family reunion, and attend a wedding while pregnant, all without buying a scrap of clothing.

Babies have this penchant for not caring about anything but eating, sleeping, and snuggling on their parents. Whether that's in a crib that three other children have already slept in or a brand-new $1,400 contraption is immaterial to them. The only person who cares what that crib looks like are the parents. If I'd spent thousands of dollars before my child was *even born*, what exactly would that portend for the rest of her life? Hundreds of dollars on a new preschool wardrobe? Thousands of dollars on school supplies for kindergarten? A pony for a seventh birthday? Start off from the perspective of spending as little as possible and you'll have more resources at your disposal to pay for the things that actually matter later on in a child's life.

Nate and I found that using secondhand baby things and eschewing the idea that more stuff makes a happier kid did not create a sense of deprivation. For us, it became not only an economical choice, but also a way of teaching our child how to value ingenuity over consumption and people over things. As we prepared for our child's birth, I realized that instead of spending time shopping, or working longer hours to earn more money to buy more stuff for our kid, Nate and I were going to circumvent that entire system and instead simply spend more time with our child. As Nate and I discussed our nascent parenting philosophy, we agreed that what kids truly need and want is time with their parents to help them learn, grow, and explore the world. For our family, thousands of dollars spent on the latest educational toys could not replace an hour-long (free) walk through the park together to explore the grass, talk about the trees, and comment on a squirrel burying a nut. Nate and I decided that what our kid needed most was us. Not us distracted and harried by jobs, struggling to pay for expensive trappings of childhood, but our presence, our imperfections, our dreams, our unique skills, our unhurried ears, and most of all, our love. Our lives were enriched and made demonstrably better thanks to our embrace of frugality. We figured that a kid would reap those same benefits.

12

That One Time We Bought a Homestead

Nate and I sat side by side on our couch, drinking coffee, scrolling through available properties in Vermont on Nate's laptop, me leaning over my baby bump to peer at the acreage listed on the screen, an exercise we'd performed for nearly two years (minus the baby bump, obviously). After scanning everything that fit our parameters on this fall day in 2015, Nate opened up a new tab, saying he'd saved one for last. It was a property in a town we'd never heard of before, in a part of the state we'd never been to, with more land and house than we'd thought we could afford. Didn't hurt that the home was gorgeous and the barn perfectly rendered. I was smitten. We had to go see it.

As we'd learned in our year and a half of searching, there weren't many places that met our criteria for a move-in-ready home and outbuilding(s), with over twenty acres of forested land, in a good school district, on a main road, not too far from a medium/large city, for under $400,000. Not that we were picky or anything . . .

Every few months, Nate and I would pop up to Vermont to tour properties with our long-suffering real estate agent. This search was a lot more laborious and tactile than our city house hunt because there are no open houses for rural homes; there's a much smaller inventory; and there are a multitude of factors to consider that don't exist in urban and suburban neighborhoods: the septic system, the well (yes, like one you get water from), the quality of the forest (since forests are a commodity), the driveway, the road, the siting of the home and outbuildings relative to the rest of the land, the presence/absence of neighbors, the acreage, the surrounding community, the distance to the grocery store—all this before ever stepping foot inside a house. Nate and I wanted to buy a property that we loved, that we could envision ourselves living on for decades to come, and perhaps for the rest of our lives. And we didn't want to overpay. And we didn't want to build new, since it's nearly impossible to recoup the expense of building on account of the site work that's required in a rural setting—digging a septic system and a well, putting in a driveway—plus the cost of the raw land to begin with. Given all this, and in spite of my advanced pregnancy, we had to go see this property.

"The map *says* there's a road here and that we're supposed to turn left on it," I relayed to Nate, not very convincingly, as he nosed the car toward what you might charitably call a footpath through pole after pole of trees. This thing was less of a road than most hiking trails I'd been on. We were driving, in that nineteen-year-old minivan, through the apparent Bermuda Triangle of rural central Vermont. It was 5 p.m. in late October 2015 and I was a full eight months pregnant. It was also raining, the sun was setting, and our gas gauge was flirting with empty, although in that car it was always hard to tell since the gauge had stopped working properly sometime after we clocked 200,000 miles. Usually you had less gas than it appeared.

We hadn't passed a house in at least fifteen minutes, we had no cell reception, and our GPS would've been more useful if we'd asked it to recite the Declaration of Independence. We came to a gravel road that was slightly larger and more prominent looking than the road we'd been on, so we decided to follow it downhill because that seemed more promising, not to mention more navigable, than going uphill. Just as I was about to get out and hike back to a farmhouse we'd seen off in the distance (over a mountain that was more of a small hill, really), we turned onto a genuine street—denoted by the fact that it was paved—and into a gas station with a deer carcass hanging in front of the Porta Potty that served as their "restroom for customers only." Aside from the terror-mingled-with-frustration we'd felt when circling for a third time onto Woodchuck Hollow Road, which was decidedly *not* paved—and, let's be honest, "road" was a generous descriptor—Nate and I were giddy. We'd just toured what I was pretty certain was our future homestead.

Back in spring 2014, we also thought we'd found our future homestead. We visited that property no less than three times with our real estate agent, the final trip with the seller and his agent as well. Our erstwhile dream home sat on sixty-nine acres of forested southern Vermont landscape with streams bisecting the woods and a pristine view of the green mountains. The home, designed by a renowned architect, was energy efficient and meticulously laid out. Efficiency appeals to Nate and me at our very core, so we were enthralled with the thoughtful footprint and modern design of the house. There was just one teeny, tiny hiccup: the interior was unfinished. And by "unfinished," I mean the floors, walls, and ceilings were clad in nothing more than plywood. Naked beams arched across the living room's cathedral ceiling (not in a trendy way), and the bathrooms had rudimentary plumbing: exposed pipes, toilets, and not much else. We spied an opportunity to finish the interior according to our tastes, with the benefit of having the expensive (and boring) site work of well, septic, foundation, roof, exterior, insulation, driveway, plumbing, and electrical already done.

Since we'd have to sink thousands into finish work, we were willing to pay only a very specific price that was pretty far south of the asking price. Securing a conventional mortgage on an unfinished house is nearly impossible, and we didn't want a construction loan because it'd hamstring us from doing the work ourselves. We made an all-cash offer, which was yet another benefit of our frugality. The seller, however, saw the house as it should be: a finished, energy-efficient *Architectural Digest* cover story. It was very much an emperor's-new-clothes scenario. In the end, we walked away. Nate and I are dreamers, but we're anchored by intense practicality. We'd offered the maximum price we were ready to write a check for, and when that was turned down, we decided this house was not for us. Our real estate agent was shocked we wouldn't stretch our budget or consider owner-financing or a construction loan, but our conviction was ironclad that we didn't want to saddle ourselves with a homestead we couldn't afford. There was no point in overspending on our dream of pursuing a simple, inexpensive life.

After this first heartbreak, we kept right on searching. We'd looked at real estate long enough to know there's never just *one* right home. It's easy to get swept up in the drama of betrothing yourself to a house, imagining where you'll put your couch and which wall you'll track your child's height on, but buying a home is as much a financial undertaking as an emotional one. In addition to in-person jaunts up to Vermont, Nate and I educated ourselves on the nuances of rural properties. Nate learned how to locate property boundaries in online maps, how to assess where power lines run (sometimes right next to the house), about different types of septic and well systems, how to determine the maturity of a forest, and more. Some of the places we considered were less than conventional, like the former commune lacking a kitchen, a half log cabin/half house that the owner had added on to, and a hunting camp with linoleum on the walls. We'd also seen quite a few attractive listings we'd seriously considered, but ultimately disqualified for various reasons: you could see the neighbors' house (we wanted to be remote), there wasn't enough acreage, there were no outbuildings, one home had a two-mile-long winding driveway leading to a house perched at the apex of a mountain (good for views but not for much of anything else), or, as happened in several instances, the surrounding town and school district weren't vibrant.

Given our year and a half of research, this newfound dream homestead seemed almost *too* good on paper, which made us fairly certain there'd be some hidden flaw. Probably it didn't have indoor plumbing or was missing half its roof or was inhabited by a family of black bears. Nevertheless, we decided to drive north for one final pre-baby homestead hunting trip, which was as much babymoon vacation as legitimate house hunt because there's no way you find your dream homestead when you're eight months pregnant with your first child, right?!

It was a chilly, clear late October day and the sky was a cloudless, brilliant, almost otherworldly blue. Most of the

trees had already completed their annual shed in preparation for winter, but enough tardy leaves remained to reward
us with a slam of vermillion or saffron or amber every few
yards. As we walked up to the house, a few of those late
leaves swirled around, crunching beneath our citified feet,
which were so accustomed to the confinement of concrete
and not the soft give of earth. The house was even better
than the pictures: fairly new construction, wide expanses of
open floor plan, four bedrooms, three bathrooms, custom
woodwork and wood floors throughout, windows on every
wall, new insulation, and no obvious faults. The real estate
agent who showed us the home clearly doubted our intentions and abilities as homestead-buyers, seeing as we were
so pregnant, so urban, and so young. Nate and I stayed
overnight at a nearby Airbnb and came back the next day
to hike the land by ourselves, which was a ritual we'd performed with every other potential homestead that'd passed
our initial inspection. We needed to feel the woods surrounding a home and be present in them on our own, since
we were making this move as much for the land as for the
house. This property was a sixty-six-acre parcel of forest,
apple trees, gardens, streams, fields, and a pond. The owners were prolific vegetable gardeners and we could see the
outline of their labors in the lower field below the house.
Bed after bed of now-dormant gardens awaited new tend-
ing. On that much land, with that much raw potential, the
possibilities were almost overwhelming.

There was a trail next to the house leading into the woods, which was a dense mix of firs and hardwoods, and we set out on it. We hiked uphill, crossing a stream, to what we calculated was the top corner of the land. I jumped up on a stump to look around. I could see acres of trees in every direction with deep autumnal hues and stark branches interrupted by the sublime green of pines. It was as beautiful as any hike in any national park. To think we could own this land—*own these woods*—was almost incomprehensible in its wonder. Hand in hand we walked back down to the house and went on a circuit through the two-acre clearing surrounding the house and barn, more city park than lawn. We found a grove of apple trees close to the house, neglected and unharvested for the season as the owners had already moved away. Nate picked two apples and we walked up to the wide, wooden-plank back porch. Sitting on that porch, with warm afternoon sun streaming down on us, eating apples from trees not fifty feet away, I started crying because I knew. This was it. This was our home. We hadn't intended to find it the month before our daughter was due. Common sense was screaming not to do it, not to make such a major decision on top of a major life change. But there was no helping it. We were hopelessly in love with this property. And the clincher? It had high-speed fiber Internet. Internet access is not a given with rural properties and this one had the crown jewel of fiber, which had been run to the house at no small expense by the previous owners and came courtesy of a nonprofit municipal collective dedicated to bringing broadband connectivity to rural central Vermont.

The next month, Nate and I alternated between conducting due diligence research on the property and a frenetic cleaning, organizing, and reorganizing of our home in preparation for our baby. We'd long since set up our entirely secondhand nursery because I had intense paranoia about the baby arriving early and us not being ready. I made Nate install the car seat when I was five months pregnant. My motto was that no one has ever regretted being overprepared for a baby. Despite our emotional attachment to this homestead, we weren't about to dive into making an offer without first running it through our own personal vetting process. Realtors can tell you only so much about a place and in the end, you're the one who has to live with the decision. Nate and I divvied up the tasks of researching both the property and the surrounding area.

We were, in the simplest terms, trying to figure out if there was a smoking gun, something sinister and wrong with this seemingly perfect property. The undertaking we were considering was substantial and amounted to a lot more than just buying a home. Some factors, such as the health of the septic system and the well, wouldn't be revealed to us until the home inspection. But there were quite a few other variables we could research on our own. There were three reasons prompting our month of exhaustive independent research:

1. We wanted to live in this home for decades and didn't want to uncover a catastrophic con *after* moving in.

2. Unlike our city home, which had appreciated tremendously over the years, we'd consider this property worth exactly $0 in our overall net worth since rural land isn't guaranteed to appreciate or even remain constant. It's not at all uncommon for houses to sit on the market for years at a time in rural locations due to a lack of demand. We never planned to get our money back on this property, so we wanted to be sure it was what we truly wanted. This wasn't a financial investment as much as it was the achievement of an emotional goal. For that reason, we wanted to be certain we loved it and could see ourselves living there for a very long time. With our Cambridge home, we'd been willing to overlook quite a few negatives because it was such a sound financial investment. We wouldn't have that knowledge to fall back on with this property.

3. The size and scope of this homestead, along with its unusual rural location, created a prodigious list of factors to take under consideration, including: the climate, our ability to maintain the quarter-mile-long driveway, the proximity of medical services, the nearest grocery store,

the community, the health of the forest, the siting of the home and barn, any legal regulations governing the property (rural land is often enrolled in a conservation or preservation program, which is usually a good thing but can hinder an owner's ability to build or change things on the property), the local school district, the churches/libraries/community services and events in the area, and of course, all the things you normally consider when buying a home, such as the construction, layout, and integrity of the structure itself.

Adding gravity to this research was the fact that our family was on the precipice of expansion and we needed to figure out if this was a place where a child could thrive. Thankfully, our years of vetting Vermont properties came in handy; we thought we knew what questions to ask. I got on the phone with the local school district, the elementary school, and the public library in an effort to suss out what types of activities were provided and how people felt about their local institutions. I asked about class sizes, arts and music, cultural events, diversity, the curriculum, and everything else I could possibly think of to ask a prospective school. To the extent possible, I wanted to know who our neighbors would be and what opportunities our child would have in this bucolic rural town. I googled doctors, dentists, pediatricians, grocery stores, and every other service I could imagine us needing to avail ourselves of. I mapped the driving distances to the nearest hospital, the nearest preschool, and more.

Meanwhile Nate hunted down foresters, lawyers who'd previously litigated on the property, and the owner once previous to the sellers. If at all possible, speaking with a previous owner of a home, but not the person trying to sell it to you, is a fabulous way to garner high-quality, unbiased, unvarnished advice. Nate's research was aimed at learning more about the sixty-six acres of land we wanted to own: what jurisdictions governed the property, how stable the forest was, and if there was anything that threw the property into an unfavorable legal light since a number of land parcels had been combined in order to create the now singly owned acreage. Our intense research turned up nothing nefarious, so we decided to move forward. It was November 23 and our due date was November 25.

We debated waiting until after the baby was born and until after the new year, perhaps, but we couldn't. The sellers had just lowered the price again and we didn't want to risk waiting. I lay on our couch with a pillow underneath my knees, hugging my bump of a baby about to be born, my feet in Nate's lap, and we deliberated. What it finally came down to after hours of research, phone calls, and Internet stalking was this question: "How would you feel if someone else bought it tomorrow?" I started crying and that settled it. We made an offer on a house, a barn, and sixty-six acres of wild, wild woods located in a deeply rural town of barely four hundred residents, the week our baby was due to join us. Because what else could we do? We'd planned, prepared, researched, and saved hundreds of thousands of dollars. This was our moment to strategically strike. There's no gain in indecision. In never taking a risk. In constantly wondering what your life would be like if you did what your heart calls you to do. Never acting on a dream is almost as bad as not having a dream in the first place.

That all sounds well and good, doesn't it? But in truth, I was terrified. Ter-ri-fied. I was about to give birth and was signing myself up for God knows what in God knows where middle of nowhere freaking deer-covered woodlands where I knew not a single soul. The closest neighbors were half a mile away. As fate would have it, I had precious little time to panic because I went into labor.

13

Birth: Something That Never Goes According to Plan

I woke up at 5 a.m. on Monday, November 30, 2015, with mild discomfort in my lower abdomen. I turned onto my side in bed and wondered what to do. I was five days past my due date, but I'd always assumed the start of labor would be accompanied by unambiguous pain, screaming, and a desire to breathe via panting. I felt none of that. It was more of a meek crampy resonance below my bump. So I googled "early labor" on my phone while Nate snoozed unaware. I saw no point in prematurely waking a man whose life was about to radically change. When our alarm went off as usual at 6 a.m., I told Nate that something was definitely happening. He leapt out of bed and asked what he should do. I told him to take the dog out and make breakfast. I had an app on my phone to track contractions, so I started punching the buttons for time and duration. I don't know how people tracked this stuff before technology. The idea of doing math at that moment in time seemed about as possible as riding in the Tour de France.

I enacted the ironclad first (and really only) part of my birth plan: take a shower. I have a thing about being clean. I once showered before going to the ER to have a softball-size sprained ankle examined, and I was absolutely showering before giving birth. The only problem was that I had to keep opening the shower door and stabbing with wet hands at my phone, which was sitting on the bathroom sink, in order to track the contractions. That charade finally over, I dressed in my going-to-the-hospital clothes, which I'd had laid out for a good month and a half, and ordered Nate into the shower. I called my doctor to explain the situation and she asked, in what I now realize was a tone of alarm, how far away from the hospital I was. It was only 7 a.m. and I'd assumed we'd be home for hours to come, days even. But she said it would be a good idea for me to come in now because, first baby or not, things were progressing rapidly. I gathered my bag (packed for weeks, naturally) and tried to eat breakfast (a ludicrous concept at this point). By now the pain had escalated to the level of confirming that this was labor, even to a neophyte laborer, and the entire ten-minute ride to the hospital, I grabbed Nate's arm and asked how far away we were (this despite the fact that I knew exactly where we were as the hospital was basically in our neighborhood). I shot eyeball daggers at all the other drivers. How could they be on the road, sipping their coffee thermoses, *listening to NPR* at a time like this?!

Ever on the lookout for savings, Nate and I had planned in advance to park the minivan somewhere on a street close to the hospital since it's in Cambridge and, as city residents, we were entitled to free street parking. This to avoid the $7 per day hospital parking garage fee. But as we neared the hospital, I used several expletives to tell Nate where he would be parking: in the parking garage in a spot closest to the door. I bolted from the car, leaving Nate to straggle in with our bags. We were met by our labor and delivery nurse, Karen, whom I am certain can only be described as an angel. Karen settled us into a birthing suite and we got comfortable, thinking we'd be there for hours.

I decided to hold off on getting an epidural since I thought natural birth was for me; after all, I'd hiked a four-thousand-foot mountain when I was six months pregnant and went to a ninety-minute heated Vinyasa flow yoga class the day before going into labor. Ten minutes later I was moaning into Karen's scrubs-covered shoulder and alternating between begging for an epidural and chewing on my bedsheet. The epidural, accompanied by an entire team, came swiftly and was every bit as magical as lore had promised. I settled into bed feeling in control again and directed Nate to text everyone I thought we could reasonably inform of our current life status. Karen and my doctor were in and out of the room, checking on me every few minutes. Meanwhile, Nate and I chatted, held hands, decided what to order for lunch (I think we were the most excited people on that entire maternity ward for the free hospital food), and took selfies.

I was feeling good, let me tell you. The contractions had subsided from their zenith of knife-stabbing-accompanied-by-a-stiletto-grinding-into-the-top-of-your-foot pain to a dull throb, which was more of a light reverberation. "Oh! Another contraction!" I'd say, instead of "Mmmmmauuuuuhhhhh," which was my pre-epidural chant. Before actually going into labor, I'd thought I'd do yoga and center myself while perhaps delivering my child into my own arms in a warm tub of water (something the hospital offered). I almost brought my yoga mat with me, thinking maybe I'd give birth while in downward dog. After going into labor, conversely, I was unwilling to even get off of the bed and was ready to administer the epidural myself. Long about 11:30 a.m., Karen reported that the baby was laboring down nicely and that I should get ready to push soon. I straightened up in bed, butterflied my legs into the one yoga pose I did manage that day, and said, "Ooooooohhhhh! *Pushing!*" Being a person who gets drunk on one glass of wine, the epidural had me positively radiant. Karen came back to check dilation a few minutes later and suddenly turned frantic. She stopped smiling, reared her head back while keeping her arm on me, and told Nate to pull the emergency call button. He did and nothing happened. It was broken. She then told him to run and get help. I was now moderately alarmed, although still feeling much like

I do after a three-champagne brunch accompanied by a small eggs Benedict. Nate, being six foot two, bearded, and imposing in the best of circumstances, apparently raised the alarm quite effectively since a phalanx of doctors and nurses streamed into our once-tranquil birthing suite, dropping clipboards and cups of coffee in their wake.

As they wheeled me away, I couldn't understand what was happening, why we were on the move, or why Karen was sitting on the bed with me. From their urgency, I gathered I should be scared. They also left Nate standing helpless in our birthing suite, which I considered a bad sign for a hospital so progressive and water-birth-encouraging as this one. All I could see was the ceiling, which was one of those drop-ceiling jobs with intersecting metal bars holding up pock-marked, white tiles. I stared and stared at it, willing it to give me answers. I kept asking if the baby was OK and then not understanding what I was being told. I couldn't make out the words. I heard the doctor yelling "faster, faster, faster." At some point, three people crowded around my head to try to make small talk. There was a wide-ranging discussion about Boston versus San Diego weather, and requests for me to squeeze someone's hand. After what felt like two hours, Nate burst through the operating room door partially clad in scrubs with his little tissue-paper hat on backward and two face masks, one to cover his beard. Then, seemingly out of nowhere, he was handed a baby. "Is that ours?" I asked. He smiled and brought the baby's face close to mine. Then they were gone and I was back to looking at the ceiling. As I learned later, I was in and out of consciousness throughout the entire cesarean section, which explains why I thought no one was answering my questions. I'd wake up long enough to shout them out and then pass out before hearing the responses.

What felt like hours as I lay there prone, unable to move, and unsure of what was happening to my body and my baby, was actually about seven minutes. After my surgery was complete, they wheeled me back into the birthing suite where Nate was standing next to the window holding what I assumed was our daughter. She didn't look like I'd thought she would. I'd imagined her all those months as a toddler, a kindergartener, a Girl Scout, but somehow not as a newborn. She was so tiny and fragile and red and mushy. But she was dazzling and beautiful. I was captivated. Nate and Karen settled her on my chest to nurse and she latched immediately, sucking away as if she were designed for this, this moment of connection and sustenance. I was the one wondering what to do, where to put my arms, whether she could breathe through her impossibly small nose that was now smashed against my chest, but she was wholly absent the anxieties of awareness. She was hungry and she knew how to eat. We lay like that for almost an hour, me sleeping, my baby eating.

When I woke up, Karen sat down next to my bed and

explained what had happened. When she'd come to check my dilation one last time before telling me to push, she'd felt what's referred to as the midwife's curse: a prolapsed umbilical cord. This means the cord was protruding ahead of the baby, which is a life-threatening situation since, if untreated, the baby will lose oxygen. Karen immediately tried the first remedy of pushing the cord back inside next to the baby, but that didn't work. The only other remedy to prevent oxygen loss, and thus extensive brain damage, is an immediate cesarean section. Karen held the cord in to ensure the baby wouldn't lose oxygen until they could cut her out. That's why her urgency was so raw and why she had Nate run screaming into the hall. Protocol was no longer important. That's why they'd whisked me off without letting Nate catch up, and why the C-section was underway before I even understood what was happening. Thanks to Karen's swift response, our daughter was born perfectly healthy, boisterous, and yelling with full lungs and an intact brain. My gratitude to Karen, our doctor, and the dozens of people who leapt into action that morning is deeper and more profound than anything I've ever felt. Cord prolapse is rare and occurs in fewer than 1 percent of pregnancies, but it doesn't feel rare when it happens to you.

Since I'd had a C-section, we'd now be in the hospital for four days as opposed to two, which sounded like a fabulous plan to me. I was exhausted, heavily drugged, and in excruciating pain. We called our parents to let them know that they were now grandparents to Estelle Juliette Thames, the middle name my grandmother's, and we told each other that the worst was over. Two days later, a doctor and a nurse woke us up in the middle of the night holding our daughter. Estelle (whom we quickly started calling Stella) had gone to the nursery for the night and while there, the nurses observed what they called "oxygen desaturation," which basically means she wasn't breathing properly and had turned blue. The doctor said they were admitting her immediately to the Level 2 NICU nursery for observation.

Estelle's minuscule hands, feet, and chest were hooked up to four different monitors to track her vital signs. These tethers meant she couldn't be more than a few feet away from her crib at any time. And so, Nate and I walked an expanse that, to me, felt like several miles from my room to the NICU every two hours so that our baby could nurse. Nate sandwiched a rocking chair in the corner behind her plastic box crib and moved the wires out of the way in order to nestle her on me to eat. Initially, the doctor planned to keep her for observation just overnight, but she continued desaturating, which kept extending her stay. She had to make it a full forty-eight hours with no desaturations before she could be discharged. While sitting in the NICU, nursing our mostly healthy, heavily monitored, full-term infant, we saw dozens of other babies in far worse condition and with dire prognoses. We felt guilty at how grateful we were and we'd grip Stella tightly any time a new infant came in, as if their malady might be contagious.

I was scheduled to be discharged after four days, but since Stella had to stay on, the hospital arranged for me to sleep in a room down the hall, not as a patient, but as a guest. My gratitude was now a deep well that kept expanding. Despite being a hospital, with all the bureaucracy that entails, they valued our desire to exclusively breastfeed and be close to our days-old child. Nate couldn't stay in the room since I had to share with another mother, so he trekked back and forth every day. He'd come at 6 a.m. and stay until 10 p.m., when I'd kick him out for fear he'd fall asleep while driving home. What I'd all but forgotten was the fact that we were in the midst of negotiating our offer on a homestead that was 150 miles away. Nate would pop out into the hospital corridor to answer calls from our real estate agent and lawyer.

He let me weave a protective cocoon around Estelle in the noisy, bright NICU while he dealt with this other looming, pressing element of our future. She and I would sleep together in the rocking chair, and invariably, one of us would shift and knock her mini foot monitor loose, setting off a peal of beeps and alarms. In spite of how often we had to have the foot monitor reattached, our nurses redefined the concept of compassion. One of them helped me shower and knelt down to wash my feet since I couldn't bend over. They brought me juice and showed me how to bathe, diaper, and nurse Estelle, which was not part of their job, but which they did with love. They could not have been more giving had I been their own daughter. On our fifth day in the NICU, two nurses popped over with huge smiles and said it was time for our photo shoot. They stuffed Stella and her many cords into a giant Christmas stocking. It was early December after all, a fact I'd forgotten. They positioned Nate and me cuddling our precious gift. At the last minute, they squirted sugar water into Stella's mouth to make her "smile." To this day, it's my favorite picture of the three of us.

After a week, Stella made it the requisite forty-eight hours with normal breathing, so we were allowed to leave. I'd become so acclimated to life in the hospital with the meals provided, the nurses there to help me, and Stella under observation so I didn't have to worry about her, that I was almost hesitant to leave. I'd come to depend on this community of people to support me. Adding to my concern was the fact that the inspection on our homestead was scheduled for 11 a.m. the day of her discharge. Nate spoke with the doctor and was able to secure a rare 6 a.m. release for us, which would give Nate just enough time to drive us home from the hospital, install us in the house, and then drive the three hours to Vermont. When we walked through the front door, I saw that Nate had arranged the living room to meet our every need. He'd lined up our three different baby bouncers and swings, laid out a gigantic pile of blankets and towels, prepared a lunch for me in the fridge, and stocked the changing table with newborn diapers (I'd bought size one diapers in advance, but Stella was a peanut who wore newborns for a good two months). I still wasn't supposed to lift anything and had a hard time sitting, standing, and walking on account of the major abdominal surgery I'd had. So I talked with my mom and sister, mothers of three children each, on the phone all day long, and gave them a minute-by-minute accounting of Stella's activities. I couldn't believe I was allowed to be alone with an infant who'd, up to this point in her life, been under constant surveillance by trained medical staff and a plethora of monitoring devices. I managed to keep her alive until Nate got home that evening and he told me our dream was a go. The homestead had passed its inspections, and we were sailing toward closing.

14

The Busiest Four Months of Our Lives

It was January 15, 2016, I was freezing, it was sleeting, we were on what was soon-to-be-our driveway of what was soon-to-be-our Vermont homestead, and we were stuck. Or more accurately, our ancient minivan was stuck. The van went *down* the quarter-mile-long, hilly, ice-covered gravel driveway fairly easily, and it'd even backed into the parking area below the driveway without incident. But now it wouldn't go back out. Nate, Stella, and I, plus Gracie the greyhound, had piled into the van at 6 a.m. that morning in Cambridge, along with an air mattress, a bassinet, a cooler of food, a box of wine (priorities), and a dog bed, and driven the three hours north to finalize the purchase of our homestead. The sellers had accepted our offer, the inspections had gone well, and here we were for the final walkthrough of the property with our real estate agent. I nursed a six-week-old Stella sitting on the staircase, then changed her diaper on the kitchen counter, while Nate checked the barn, the tractor (which was included in the sale), and the house to ensure everything was in order and that the sellers had performed the two repairs we'd requested: fixing the master bathroom toilet and installing a radon-mitigation system in the basement. Finding no flaws, we loaded our menagerie back into the van (no small feat, since the dog was supposed to sit next to the baby in the backseat and was forever overdoing her jump into the car and landing on the car seat).

Nate turned the engine and we felt the tires skid underneath us. There was too much ice for our snow-tireless van. After our real estate agent put some dirt under the wheels, we were able to squeal out of our parking spot. Nate gunned it up three-quarters of what was about to be our driveway, but the van surrendered on the final hilly crest that weaves around a tree just before you reach the road. We'd known this driveway would be a pain because it was steep and long and our sole responsibility to maintain. But the pros of this homestead—the land, the gorgeous house, the pond, the high-speed fiber Internet, and the good school district—all outweighed it. Or so we'd thought. The minivan was now entrenched on this hill like a dowager ensconced in her chair during a wedding reception's devolution into the chicken dance, unwilling to move in either direction. Nate got out to hike back down to the house to ask our real estate agent to call a tow truck since, naturally, we had no cell reception. Sitting in the passenger seat, I turned up NPR and the heat and reached into the backseat to pat the girls. As I hummed along to the *Morning Edition* theme song, the van started sliding backward on the ice. I jumped out of the car and released a primordial scream—the scream that mothers over millennia have screamed when their babies were about to be eaten by a woolly mammoth/succumb to the plague/slide off an icy driveway. I started to run behind the van to stop it with my body when Nate jogged up the driveway and grabbed me to prevent me from being run over. The van gently slid into a snowbank on the side of the driveway and came to a smooth stop. I ripped Stella out of the car and sat in the snow sobbing hysterically. In the span of fifteen seconds, all the confidence I'd built this past month and a half that we were doing the right thing, that this homestead was the one, that we weren't crazy to move to the middle of nowhere with an infant, was shattered. Obliterated.

I felt stupid, and not just for trying to bolt behind a moving car as opposed to climbing over into the driver's seat to steer like a rational person. We knew this twenty-year-old minivan that lacked all-wheel drive and snow tires wasn't optimal for driving in snow, but we'd done it anyway. As Nate held me holding Stella in the fifteen-degree air on the side of the driveway, our Vermont-native real estate agent managed to drive the car out of the driveway in what can only be described as a cannonball run. I cried and shook the entire drive to our lawyer's office for the formal closing and paperwork signing. Nate asked if I still wanted to go through with it. I hesitated. This episode encapsulated all my fears about this move: that we'd be out of our depth on such rural land, that we weren't prepared, and that there'd be no one to help me if something happened to our baby. However, we'd spent so much time researching this decision that, despite my misgivings, I was confident this was the place. I also considered the alternative of not following this dream, of returning to the city, of living with all-encompassing regret. That was an even worse fate. So I said yes, but with the caveat that I never wanted to drive that car down that driveway ever again. And we didn't.

It was now a full hour past our scheduled appointment time with our lawyer, the seller, a banker, and both real estate agents. We burst into the office a hot mess: me having only recently stopped crying, Stella in a carrier snuggled against my chest in her best imitation of a marsupial, and Nate clutching our sixty-pound dog who was wild-eyed from the trauma of riding in a car and climbing up the three flights of stairs to the office. I'm pretty sure they all thought we were crazy. Not crazy in a fox-type way, but genuinely out of our minds. The papers were signed as our dog panted on the floor and Stella nursed, the keys were handed over, and we even remembered to have our real estate agent snap a family photo of us.

That night we parked the van at the top of the driveway and hiked down to the house in the dark, lit by the flashlights I'd thrown into the car at the last minute. Camping out in our new home, with a fire glowing in the woodstove and Stella snoozing on her bassinet mattress on the floor, Nate and I toasted with the box of wine we'd brought and agreed that this was, in fact, it. We'd done it. Or at least the first part of it, because that night was the start of the busiest four months I've ever endured. We'd be moving up to Vermont full time in May and before that happened, we needed to buy two cars and I needed to quit my job; we needed to rent out our Cambridge house, have Nate work full time at his office, build up my freelance business, and pack up all of our worldly possessions. With an infant.

"Replace minivan" had been sitting on our to-do list for some time, but after its performance on the driveway, we hurried that line item along. Moving to the woods from the city wasn't merely a change in scenery, it was a sweeping lifestyle revamp; we needed two reliable cars instead of one geriatric van. There's no public transit in rural Vermont, and we had no desire for one of us to be unable to leave the property if the other was out. Nate had been doing car research for years so that when the time came, we'd be prepared to buy. That spring, we paid cash for a used Subaru Outback and a used Toyota Prius, which allowed us to achieve our dual goals of excellent gas mileage (via the hybrid Prius) and all-wheel drive (via the Subaru) for Vermont's snow and mud seasons.

Paying cash in full for two cars just three months after having our first child and a month after buying a homestead without needing to first sell our Cambridge home was our extreme frugality in action. We'd saved for years by forgoing unnecessary luxuries and economizing on necessities so that we could do exactly this: spend on the things that mattered to us. Also, I'd be remiss if I didn't point out that buying a new car has to be one of the worst financial decisions humanly possible. Cars depreciate the minute—yes the *minute*—they're driven out of the showroom, and the markup on a new car is egregious. A used car, on the other hand, allows you to let someone else suffer that initial depreciation while you get a vehicle that's still perfectly safe, drivable, and vastly less expensive. Want real numbers? Here you go: in 2016, we bought a 2010 Subaru Outback with 100,000 miles for $12,000 and a Toyota Prius, also a 2010 and also with just under 100,000 miles, for $9,000. Brand new in 2010, that Outback retailed for $26,790 and the Prius for $23,800. That means we realized a 55 percent discount on the Subaru and a 62 percent discount on the Prius. We spent $21,000 total on two reliable cars that were just six years old and in excellent condition, versus the staggering $50,590 price tag of new. And don't fool yourself into thinking you need a new car for the safety features or the all-wheel drive, because you can find all these amenities and more in cars that are just a few models earlier than the current.

Owning a car at all is a luxury, and I'm of the belief that all luxuries, from chocolate to elective home renovations, should be paid for in full and with cash. If you can't pay cash? You don't get to buy it. In the spirit of keeping the cycle of used cars alive, we sold our 1996 Honda Odyssey minivan for $1,000 on Craigslist in Cambridge because it was still a great car, just not a car equipped for life in the rural wilds. That resale illustrates another cardinal truth about used cars: you can usually resell them at a rate that nets you a fairly reasonable return on your initial investment. You probably won't make all of your money back, but since the initial, colossal depreciation already took place, your resale price will be much closer to the price you paid. This as opposed to the remarkable discrepancy between the price of a new car and its resale potential.

Paying cash for cars is also a perfect illustration of the fact that frugality is a compounding game. By never having car payments or any other non-mortgage debt, and the often-exorbitant interest rates that go along with such debt, Nate and I have always been able to save at a high rate, which means we're able to avoid having car payments, which means we're able to save at a higher rate . . . it's a virtuous cycle of low spending and high saving that's self-perpetuating. The less money you need to live on, the more you save, and the less you need to earn. Plus, when you're paying off a car loan or other debt with interest, your money is compounding in your creditor's favor. When you instead invest that money in low-fee index funds, for example, your money is working for you and compounds in *your* favor. And it doesn't take all that much money to yield substantial dividends in the future. Since I've already gone there, let's do another example with real numbers. For this exercise, I'm going to use cable television, which has to be my all-time favorite budget scapegoat.

Here's the premise: Would you rather watch TV or have $91,000? Permit me to explain. Let's say you spend $75 a month on cable. I'll grant you that doesn't sound like a huge amount of money on its own. But multiplied by twelve months, that's $900 a year on television. Now, let's say you instead invested that $900 in low-fee index funds and realized a 7 percent return, which is considered an average annual market return over the long term. Imagine you kept that same $900 invested for decades, which is the wisest way to invest, and added $900 to your investments every year instead of paying for cable. *In thirty years, your annual investments of $900 would've grown to $91,865.74. Yeah, you read that right: $91,865.74.* Now ask yourself again: Would you rather have $91K or watch television?

That is the power of frugality (coupled with diligent investing) to transform your net worth. When you turn your money over to someone else, a cable company for example, you're not just giving up that dollar amount, you're giving up all of the potential gains that money could have for you. In other words, the opportunity cost. And that was an example using *just one* useless monthly bill totaling a measly $900 per year. Imagine what the total would be in thirty years if you eliminated haircuts, movies at the theater, manicures, new clothes, new furniture, takeout, new cars, lattes, and everything else that's a drain on your monthly expenses. The heart of extreme frugality is the knowledge that the compilation of seemingly piddly amounts of money yield tremendous dividends over time. It's not like Nate and I have been invested for thirty years yet; we were only thirty-two years old at the time; but we'd saved at such a high rate that we'd walked our way right out of the culture of more and right into financial independence. Nearly anyone with a decent job could do what we've done, yet very few do. Why? Because it takes short-term sacrifice, long-term planning, and a conviction that what we want out of life isn't sold in a store.

I want to take a step back for a moment and acknowledge the privilege inherent to our situation. Although Nate and I didn't inherit money and our parents didn't fund our adulthood or buy us a house, we're both profoundly privileged. We made some good financial decisions, sure, but we also got supremely lucky and, in many ways, the game was rigged in our favor. We were raised by well-educated, financially and emotionally stable parents who taught us to read, made sure we went to school, and shepherded us through life. These parents helped us pay for college and gave us advice on how to write our first résumés and did practice job interviews with us. The deck was stacked in our favor before we were even born. Our financial advantages are the product of our socioeconomic status, our education levels, and most of all, the benefits we both had while growing up. I believe that people—Nate and me included—aren't successful simply because they've made a few good decisions. I never want to lose sight of the fact that privilege courses through our lives and that Nate and I would be nowhere without this lucky start. We were born in the right country at the right time to the right people. All beyond our control, yet all largely responsible for where we are today. There's a great deal of institutional privilege and straight-up luck that goes into the success Nate and I have enjoyed.

Amid these sound financial decisions and ability to pay cash for used cars and math about cable TV and the fulfillment of our dreams, Nate and I were mired in the often baby-spit-up-covered, often sleep-deprived, often harried trenches of our four months of insanity. As if it weren't enough to parent a three-month-old, buy cars, and rent out and pack up a home, Nate and I experienced a string of homeowner nightmares (all in our Cambridge house) that we've come to call Revenge of the Appliances. I wish this were hyperbolic, but it's pretty much not. First, one of the pipes in our Cambridge home froze and burst on a particularly frigid night, which we discovered after arriving home at 8 p.m. on a Sunday after a weekend in Vermont. Nate taught himself how to install PEX plumbing and replumbed our entire kitchen at 10 p.m. Next our oven broke. Nate took it apart, replaced several pieces, put it back together, and it still didn't work. We called oven repair people who did the exact same thing and it still didn't work. We bought a new oven. The closet door in our master bedroom came off of its rolling track and we had to dismantle, repair, and reassemble it. Our main water valve wouldn't shut off all the way and had to be replaced, which necessitated turning the water off to our entire street one morning. We had to replace two upstairs ceilings that threatened to collapse. The downstairs bathtub required refinishing. A hole in the floor needed fixing. And the Subaru's windshield broke, which necessitated replacement. Also something happened to our toilet; Nate did something to make it all better. Our freezer started dripping water into our fridge, which was DIY-able after considerable time spent on diagnostics. I also interviewed property managers for our soon-to-be-rental as well as moving companies for our soon-to-occur-move and contractors for those two ceilings, which had to be demolished and installed afresh . . . and then needed crown molding to conceal the gap created between the old walls and the new ceilings. Not to mention the bottomless reams of paperwork and logistics surrounding moving (see me picking up free moving boxes from my Buy Nothing group), becoming landlords (see me cleaning the house in preparation for it to be photographed and rented out), two new cars (see me at the DMV getting licenses and registrations), and welcoming a new human to the universe (see me in line at City Hall buying copies of her birth certificate).

I always like to think that I can do anything for a short period of time and, in retrospect, this seems like a hilarious rundown of mishaps; but at the time, I was exhausted and nearly burnt to a crisp. I was figuring out how to be a parent, Nate was still working at an office all day every day, stuff kept breaking in the house we were trying to rent out, we had another house 150 miles away that we drove up to check on every weekend, and I forgot to mention that I was also growing my online business. We'd decided long before finding our homestead that I wouldn't go back to my nine-to-five job after my maternity leave ended. I'd been building Frugalwoods in addition to my day job for two years at that point, and writing freelance articles for other financial sites. That fall, we'd realized Frugalwoods was a *thing* and an actual revenue-generating business. Next to birthing my child, I was birthing this passion project that let me espouse my beliefs about frugality and simple living. And it was working. People were reading it! Lots of people! But the thing about a baby and a business is that they both need to be fed. Fortunately, I could multitask these dual needs. I'd snuggle Stella on top of a pillow (a hand-me-down My Brest Friend, if you must know) and wedge her between my body and the kitchen table so that she could nurse while I worked on my laptop. It was an epitome of the third way that Nate and I were carving out. We didn't want to outsource our daughter's care—not to mention the fact that daycare in Cambridge costs more than our mortgage—but we also didn't want to give up doing work that was meaningful to us. I don't work because we need the money. Our frugality allowed me to quit that lifestyle before I turned thirty-two. I work because *I enjoy it*. Because it enriches me and brings deeper fulfillment to my days.

May 2016 finally arrived, we had tenants and a signed lease for an amount of rent that was revenue-generating after expenses, and we were miraculously packed and ready to go a full three days before a moving truck and my blessed in-laws showed up at our house to schlep me, Nate, one dog, one baby, a household full of (mostly used) material possessions, and two cars from urban to rural.

15

Our Third Way

It was July 4, 2016, and I'd signed up to bring three watermelons and two pies. Nate was down for setting up tents and "chicken hauling," despite uncertainty over what the latter entailed. The parade started at 10 a.m., so at 9:45 I drove Stella the two miles from our house to the town center. I entrusted the pies and watermelons to the ladies' auxiliary, who were assembling the chicken lunch in the kitchen of our town center building. As I walked across the sun-drenched street to the pastoral lawn of what serves as our town's library, children's activity center, store selling locally made goods, coffee shop, hostel, and home to such groups as the Civics Klatch, the Women's Wellness Circle, and the Historical Society, I waved to Nate, who was setting up tents with a few of our neighbors.

I bought a shortcake from the library's strawberry shortcake fund-raiser and settled in on the lawn with friends to watch the parade. Stella was soon swooped into the arms of one of our neighbors and I chatted with another mom I'd recently met. With a siren blast from our volunteer fire department's truck, the parade was under way. All the kids in town led the parade riding bikes they'd decked that morning with ribbons, stickers, and balloons. There was also a contingent wearing what I assume were last year's very patriotic Halloween costumes: an Abe Lincoln, a Lady Liberty, and a dinosaur wearing an American flag hat. Our local state rep and his wife drove in their truck and waved. The parade was all of five minutes long, but the cheers were riotous. Afterward, the kids re-collected the candy they'd thrown to the parade spectators (aka their parents and the other adults in town). Stella and I met up with Nate, who'd completed his tent-setting-up duty and was getting ready to chicken haul, which as it turned out meant toting chickens from the outdoor roaster inside to the kitchen for the luncheon. We'd lived in Vermont for barely two months and we already knew more people and had a more gratifying community life than we'd ever had in the city.

Back in Cambridge, and before that in DC and New York City, we'd been surrounded by people. Our neighbor's house in Cambridge was a mere ten inches away from ours. The buses, the subways, and the sidewalks were glutted with humanity. But we hardly knew anyone. We had a set of friends we'd get together with periodically for dinner parties or game nights, but we didn't have a true community. Our Vermont town of four hundred people, on the other hand, embodies that word. People here are self-sufficient, because you have to be to live this remotely. They chop their own wood, grow their own food, and raise their own livestock, but they're also interdependent. They know no one can do it all alone so they lean on one another. Back in the city, I'd always say things to friends along the lines of, "You should stop by sometime" or "Let me know if you need help with anything," but my words were empty and people rarely took me up on my offer. The first time I said something along those lines to a neighbor here in Vermont, they were in my garden the next morning helping me dig out flower bulbs to donate to the town's plant, book, and bake sale fund-raiser.

I didn't know I was missing—lacking, even—the warmth, the support, and the wisdom that a community offers until we moved to Vermont. The day after we moved in, as Nate and I scrambled to unpack, a woman appeared at our back door. After living in the often-contentious close quarters of cities for years, my first thought was that we'd already done something to offend the neighbors and that she was here to complain and/or inform us we were being sued. But this is not the city and that was not the case. Rather, she'd heard we'd moved in and had stopped by to give us several jars of homemade jam and to ask if we needed anything. Dumbstruck, we invited our new neighbor inside and chatted for an hour. This stereotypically rural behavior repeated itself as neighbor after neighbor dropped by unannounced to offer us a homemade foodstuff, assistance, and a keen interest in shooting the breeze. After each of our new friends departed, Nate and I would turn to each other and say, "This is why we moved here! This is what we wanted!" Connection, warmth, and community-minded spirit. I'm no longer surprised by the immense kindness of everyone I meet out here, but I'm touched every time.

About six months after moving in, one of my neighbors asked if she could come over to watch our daughter. I initially thought she was offering her services as a babysitter, which sounded good, but she quickly clarified that she didn't want to be paid. Without putting it in so many words, she wanted to become Stella's adopted grandmother. Our neighbor doesn't have grandchildren of her own yet and she adores children. Seeing that Nate and I didn't have any family living nearby, she intuited that we'd probably welcome the help, warmth, and ultimately the love that a grandparent provides. She now comes over one morning a week to watch Stella, and one evening a month to allow Nate and me to go out on a date.

This is a remarkable gift to us new parents, which is made all the more special because she's not a blood relative and she doesn't owe us this service. She doesn't have to love our daughter, but she does. I know that arrangements like this exist in cities, in suburbs, and everywhere else, but for me, this type of deep connection didn't happen before our Vermont life. Not many people live out here, so those that do tend to forge relationships that defy market forces and social norms. There's documented research in behavioral economics that people don't respond well to being paid for what they consider favors to friends, and I find that rings particularly true in our rural community. Not much money changes hands, but a great deal of work gets shared around, which is how Nate found himself helping to fix the well at the town community center one Tuesday. And how he finds himself serving on the boards of two different local nonprofit organizations. And why every gathering out here is a potluck, weddings included.

Another unique and fulfilling aspect of our rural life that I appreciate is the intergenerational relationships that form. When I lived in cities, I found that I always gravitated toward people who were almost exactly my age. Outside of work colleagues, I don't think I had a single friend who didn't fall within a few years of my birth date. Here in Vermont, however? I have friends ranging in age from nine to ninety. I never realized how much I was missing out on in my social life by having such a narrow age bracket of friends. I recently went to a double birthday party for two of my friends from church who were turning thirty and seventy, and it wasn't until we were singing happy birthday and watching their heads bow over their candles—one gray with wisdom, one red with youth—that I understood the power of cross-generational friendships. For starters, these people know a lot of stuff! Nate and I joke that he should establish a weekly meeting with our sixty-year-old neighbor across the street because Nate ends up calling him every few days seeking his advice on some aspect of planting our vegetable garden, or what to do with ashes from our woodstove, or where to buy chainsaw parts. Learning from our older neighbors and enjoying the richness of their experiences is one of my favorite aspects of my new life.

What I didn't understand before experiencing this level of all-encompassing, interdependent community is that our consumer culture has tried to do away with the essence of community. Coffee shops, restaurants, clothing stores, computer brands, and more have all co-opted our inherent human desire for community. For belonging. For a tribe. Our modern world has dismantled our previously tight-knit communities of family members and neighbors bound together by the necessities of remote, agrarian life. It's now much more common to drive to work alone in our car every morning, work all day in front of a computer screen, return home after dark, spend a few hours with our immediate family, then repeat that pattern over and over again. That's what Nate and I did for years. There's no time to meet our neighbors, let alone help them spread mulch in their vegetable garden in exchange for tomatoes. We're taught we can pay for everything we need. Our very lives can be purchased, and by extension, we can buy the rights to a fragmented community of like-minded consumers. Our unifying activity as a culture is shopping, and the one thing we all are is consumers. Consumption has become our spiritual outlet, our means of building relationships, of identifying ourselves by the brands emblazoned on our clothes, cars, shoes, laptops, and it has supplanted our interpersonal dependencies.

Here in rural Vermont, however, I've found a group of people who consciously disavow mainstream culture. There are no malls or movie theaters in our town. Instead, there are monthly town-wide potlucks; coffee hour (with homemade coffee and goodies) every Saturday morning at the library/local shop/community center; contra dances on the weekends; neighbors coming over to help with the maple syruping or the apple harvesting; town festivals and celebrations; a free summer camp for kids; the knowledge that you can stop by a neighbors' house unannounced; the security that your kids are watched over by a wide net of people and that if they misbehave you'll hear about it; and a sense that we do, in fact, need one another. Not everyone is best friends out here, but most people would help you out of a ditch in mud season without expecting anything in return. The culture harkens back to a Rockwellian Americana I'd assumed was dead; but it's not, it's just slightly altered since many of us out here make our living at least in part via the Internet.

Our first week on the homestead, I felt like I was still running the marathon of our previous four months. Since my in-laws generously came to help us move and were watching Stella, Nate and I blitzed through unpacking and had the whole house set up in two days. We stashed everything unnecessary in the basement because I'd decided that in this house—in this new practice of simple living—I wanted to unpack only the things we used on a daily basis. I didn't want throw pillows on our bed anymore because all they did was waste my time and clutter up our space. I started to apply the principles of minimalism that guided my spending to the physical objects in my home. As soon as the last box was unpacked, Nate and I ran (I actually remember us jogging) outside to tackle the weeds in our bed of asparagus, planted by a previous owner and growing despite the jungle trying to choke the tender green stalks. We carried on like this for several weeks, corybantically jumping from one project to the next: repairing culverts, digging trenches, chopping firewood, weeding garden beds. Exhausted and overwhelmed by the scope of outdoor work that all seemed to need our attention right away, Nate and I realized we had to stop. We'd been on this treadmill of *doing* in order to get here and we needed to relish it. At a certain point, you have to stop striving and start living. You have to arrive.

One warm June evening after we put Stella to bed, I got out our Scrabble board, poured two glasses of wine, and went out on the back porch with Nate. As we played and chatted instead of working on the land, which we'd done every other night, we started to sink into gratitude. Into a recognition of how incredibly fortunate we were to achieve this unusual dream at such a young age and to have the rest of our lives to enjoy it. We weren't going to get it all done that first year: the vegetable gardens we'd dreamed of, the firewood we needed to chop, the chickens we hoped to raise, the hiking trails we wanted to build through our woods, the apple cider we wanted to make, the bridge over the outlet to our pond that needed repairing (still does, come to think of it . . .). It wasn't all going to happen. And that was OK. Living on sixty-six acres means signing up to never be bored, to never have a dearth of projects, to never need to pay for entertainment, all of which we wanted. We had to ease into the realization that this life and this home-stead was one of opportunity and one of balance, not a sprint of getting things done. As we talked this over, our mind-set shifted and we started to live with abundant grat-itude instead of desperation over what was still undone. We started a routine of taking a hike together as a family every day, a practice we continued year-round, even in the depths of winter with snowshoes on our boots and Stella pulled behind us in a sled. Being in our woods transforms me every single time; after all, it's why we came here in the first place. Without fail, I breathe more easily and am refreshed after time spent in nature. Joy is not a "done" to-do list; rather, it's the ability to appreciate and savor the simplicity of each day's routine. To not feel that you need a vacation from your life. To know that you're living as close to your ideal as possible, every single day.

After coming to the realization that we were no longer

beholden to the hectic modern mind-set of ticking down lists, Nate and I created a new rhythm of life. I've come to think of it as our own personal third way. For starters, we never set an alarm clock. We're also not any one thing all the time—homesteaders, people who work on the Internet, parents—but we're an amalgamation of these facets of our lives. We wanted diversity in our days, and now we have it. There is no handbook for what we do, this life that encompasses so many different niches, so we get to experiment, fail, succeed, and experiment again. What I've learned is that there are many other options for how a life can operate beyond the narrow, pigeonholed ruts our culture tries to force each of us into. Your goal is likely not to move to a homestead in the woods of Vermont (although, hey, maybe it is!), but what I've found is that most people want more out of life than simply slogging through it as a mindless consumer. Whatever your goal happens to be, managing your money wisely and taking charge of how you spend it is one of the first steps in allowing something new and different and wonderful to flourish in your life.

Nate and I used our money in unconventional ways for years; now, we applied those same lessons to how we used our time. Just as our consumer culture offers a full range of ways to spend our money, it also prescribes how we should use our time. We're supposed to go to college, get jobs, get married, buy a house, have kids, and enroll in the idea that we'll have to do this for the next forty years or more.

That we'll have to work to earn money to support a lifestyle we're expected to have, because that's what everyone else does. But it's not the only way. It is so easy to accidentally let other people dictate your life; it happens to most of us without our even realizing it. We get slotted into predetermined roles based on societal expectations, something I did for years, without considering how *we'd* spend our time and money if we had the freedom to choose.

Nate and I also chart a third, nontraditional path in the way that we balance work and family: we both work and we both stay home with our daughter every day and have no paid childcare providers. We've blurred the lines between the standard dichotomy of stay-at-home parent versus working parent. We are both. This unusual arrangement is now feasible for some families given the Internet, the ability to work remotely, and the unconventionality inherent to entrepreneurship and modern marriages/partnerships. But it requires ruthless prioritization of how you use your time and your money: both must go only in service of what matters most to you. When our daughter goes down for a nap, no matter what else is happening that day, I sit down and write. I can be found writing with baby spit on my clothes and in my hair, with the washing machine singing its end-of-cycle song, and with dirty dishes stacked so high the faucet won't turn on. But that is my ruthless prioritization, and that is what allows me to be home with my daughter and my husband while pursuing a career I'm passionate about. Now, on a practical level, let me be clear: it's not possible for both parents to work full time every day, but a balance does exist. It's unconventional, but then what in my life isn't?

Nate and I choose to work for the intellectual fulfillment, not because we need the income, and I'm keenly aware of the privilege inherent to our situation. I'm also conscious that our frugality is elective, as opposed to mandatory, and that Nate and I are fortunate beyond belief to be in this position. Our conviction that we're privileged is one of the motivators behind our decision to create a donor advised fund through which we contribute annually to charities. We feel an imperative to give back financially as well as through volunteer work in our community. While there are elements of our lifestyle that are purely choices of personal responsibility, the overarching trajectory we find ourselves on is heavily weighted by our upbringings, our educations, and our resulting earning power. Although we never made investment banker salaries, and in fact both worked for nonprofit/mission-based organizations, we made good money. And the more you earn, the more you can save and the quicker you can reach financial independence. That's not to say that it can't be done on lower salaries or with fewer built-in privileges, merely that the road was easier for Nate and me. Despite this, I don't want you to feel discouraged if your circumstances are different from mine, because there are gains to be had anywhere along the spectrum of frugality. For some folks, paying down debt will provide that peace of mind; for others, it's having a lifetime of savings invested in the market; for others, it's the ability to pay cash for their children's higher education. In whatever way you define financial security and peace, frugality is a tool that will get you there faster.

In addition to our balance between parenting and working, Nate and I both crave a balance between work that's cerebral, done between our fingertips and a keyboard, and work that's physical, done across wide swaths of our property. Achieving that synergy between physical and mental is perhaps my favorite aspect of life on our homestead. I write on my laptop, looking out the window at our apple orchard, until there are no more words. Then, depending on the season, I go outside and pull weeds from our vegetable garden or pick blackberries from the tsunami of bushes that grows wild and unchecked on the perimeter of our woods. Or I take Stella on a snowshoe hike through folded layers of whipped-cream snow. Nate, for his part, bangs away at ones and zeros (this, apparently, being what software engineers do) until he needs to move. And then I see him from the window, pruning our apple trees or in the woods with his chainsaw bringing down a tree for firewood, splitting it by hand with a maul, and stacking it in rows to dry for the winter. In the city, our lives were divorced from the natural world. It didn't matter if it was snowing, or 95 degrees, or if blackberries were ripe somewhere; we were in offices all day long no matter what. Now, we base our days around seasonality. Each month, each day, even, blasts us with the minutiae of seasonal imperatives. The first few weeks of living here, we harvested rhubarb constantly as it was in the height of its growing season and I could not fathom what we'd do with so much rhubarb. But then, just as quickly, the plants turned inward and became dormant (being a neophyte gardener, I thought they were dead). Their time was done. My first lesson in the impermanence of a season. Having an intimate relationship with the natural world is a liberation from the technology, the pressures, the conformity, and the consumer-driven lifestyle of our modern age. Out here, it's not about us, it's about the seasons, the weather, the woods. We're not in control and I love it. This new iteration of life is still evolving for us and will be for some time, I imagine. Our family is young, our homesteading knowledge is nascent, and we see a languid unfurling of maturation awaiting us in every sense. The unknowns of this future thrill me.

16

Smoothing Out the Happiness Curve

The idea is to cut the saplings as close to the ground as possible. Same goes for the brushy weeds and twiggy stems. I was wielding the clippers, Nate had the handsaw, and Stella was asleep in a hand-me-down Ergo attached to my chest. We were chopping our way through the trail next to our house; in fact, the very same trail we hiked up when deciding to buy our property. Nate later took the chainsaw and removed the logs bisecting the path, making this our first official cleared hiking trail. It extends in a loop circumnavigating our land at its perimeter, starting and ending at our house. In the summer months, we put Stella in the carrier and take our clippers on each hike, beating back the incessant undergrowth scheming to overtake our footpath. For winter hiking, we got a game sled, traditionally used by hunters to cart deer and other game from the woods, lined it with blankets, and nestled Stella inside. Sleds specially designed to tow kids are four times the price and not as durable for handling rough terrain. Nate and

I strap on snowshoes and Stella snoozes while we pull her through our snow-covered woods. We can hike any day of the year, right outside our front door, and most days, we do. There's no longer a barrier to entry and we don't have to drive for hours or plan ahead or take the day off work. The woods are simply there for us.

It's true that Nate and I don't buy Christmas, birthday, or anniversary gifts for each other. But it's equally true that we don't need to. We've smoothed out the happiness curve of our lives. Rather than living for vacations or weekends, we've created a life that delivers ongoing happiness on a daily basis. Before embracing extreme frugality, our lives resembled a spiky graph with peaks denoting milestones— our wedding, dinners out on Saturday nights, weekend getaways—followed, inevitably, by the lowest valleys. Those ever-present valleys represented our daily routine, the Monday-through-Friday sludge of cubicles and office politics. We'd offset those valleys by spending money. By treating ourselves. And while sure, there were the euphoric highs of buying a new dress or having a sumptuous meal out, we spent most of our time at our baseline, down in the valleys. Through frugality, Nate and I elevated our baseline to a permanent state of contentment. We're not deliriously gleeful every day, but our graph trends upward and is mostly smooth. We still have occasional spikes—a vacation, say—but on the whole, what we've done is create a daily routine that embodies the things we love. Nate and

I used to work for the weekend, for our two days of escapism. Now, we're orchestrating a life where every day is an honest deliverance of our passions. Rather than work jobs we don't enjoy in order to afford hits of consumerism to soothe the discontent we feel over working those jobs, we stepped out of that loop entirely.

Our culture espouses a "treat yourself" mentality that goads us to surrender to all the short-term goodies we can possibly conceive of: lattes, Netflix, a new car. We deserve it, right? But I think the "treat yourself" culture masks a deep-seated fear that we'll never realize our long-term dreams, so we'd better live it up in the present. This becomes a self-fulfilling prophecy. The more we buy now, the less money we have to make actionable progress toward our dreams later. The instantly gratifying thrills that our consumer culture peddles—everything from snack delivery services to biting-fish pedicures—are nothing more than road-bump opiates: short-term pleasures that only serve to derail our actual goals. And we don't apply this mentality just to tiny purchases. If we think we'll never save up enough for a down payment on a house, we might be more liable to rent a ritzy apartment and fritter away our would-be down payment savings. I'm astounded at how many ways there are to waste money, and at how many of them I've personally fallen victim to. Marketers diligently create needs we never knew we had and many products advertised to us fill false needs. This type of spending skirts the question of what we really want out of life. It's the classic conundrum of forgoing delayed gratification played out day after day, purchase after purchase. The more we buy, and buy into this culture of more, the more we think we need. It's a vicious, endless cycle.

While I'm pretty sure the phrase "extreme frugality" sounds like a penance, it's actually the exact opposite. It's a deliverance. Nate and I consider our lives to be luxurious: we live where we want, as we want, on our own terms, and we're not beholden to anyone else. If that's not luxury, I don't know what is. Sure, we don't have new cars, but the key is that we don't want new cars or need new cars. We view money as a tool to be spent on things we need and that we value highly. Money doesn't bring us happiness, but it has granted us the financial freedom to construct a life we love.

It's also true that Nate and I are satisfied with less. We've discovered that the rarity of something's occurrence serves to enhance its enjoyment. Just like eating to excess or drinking to excess, spending to excess delivers no lasting fulfillment. Judiciously meting out the resource of money, on the other hand, allows us to relish the things we do buy. When Nate and I go out to dinner, an infrequent event, we savor each bite. We thoroughly enjoy ourselves and we appreciate the uniqueness of the experience. Frugality turned us into people who feel profound gratitude for everything we have, as opposed to the people we used to be, constantly scraping and grasping for more.

We've also simplified nearly every aspect of our lives. Instead of looking for expensive solutions, Nate and I ask ourselves what can we stop doing, stop needing, and stop buying. I've stopped painting my nails, stopped wearing makeup, stopped fixing my hair, and just generally stopped doing stuff that ate up my time without delivering a commensurately valuable return on my investment.

We try to identify the root of the issue and the problem we're trying to solve, as opposed to what a consumer mind-set would tell us to buy. We live in a culture where people are lured into buying things they don't need to fill houses that are too large and then feel compelled to move to ever-larger houses and work ever-longer hours in order to support a life that they're barely living. A life that they perhaps did not consciously choose, and that they perhaps do not even extract pleasure from.

"But I don't want to live in the woods and I like my job." I hear this from readers all the time, to which I respond: it's not about wanting to move to the woods or quit your job. It's about liberating yourself from reliance on the salary that your job provides. Nate and I both choose to continue working to this day because we derive satisfaction from our work. The salient point is that we have the option to quit at any time. To walk away and pursue a different avenue in life. If we were instead wholly dependent on the money we're paid for this work, our options would be much more limited or nonexistent. In addition to the freedom this provides, it's also a hedge against calamity and a way of self-insuring. If something terrible were to befall us—from a catastrophic illness to a car that won't start—money would not be an issue. There are a multitude of things in this life that we cannot predict, or prevent, or plan for, but financial stability is something that is largely within our control. I prefer to shore up my resources while I can in defense of the future unknowns. This doesn't make me a fatalist, but a pragmatic realist. Life is easier to cope with when you have enough money. Control what you can and the rest of life becomes much less complicated to navigate.

You very well might work your job for the next forty years and love it every day, and I know plenty of people who have. However, no one has ever regretted having more money in retirement than they planned for: you can endow your grandchildren's higher education, you can start a private foundation and donate to charity, and you can travel the world year-round. It's also true that we live in mercurial times where jobs and pensions are not the bulwarks of security they once were. While none of us thinks we'll ever be laid off, it's no longer a certainty in most professions. Saving money now ensures you'll be able to take advantage of the opportunities, and manage the hurdles, that life will inevitably throw in your path. As Nate and I discovered when we unexpectedly found our homestead ahead of schedule, there's nothing more liberating than wanting to pursue an unusual dream and having the financial ability to do so.

After nearly four years of dedicated extreme frugality, I've come to realize there are stages of frugal adherence. I've now arrived at what I imagine to be the final stage: profound contentment. I've freed myself from stressing out about my appearance, about my furniture, about my success. I've let go of the nagging external prompts to buy more and to, in the process, change who I am. I quite like who I am, and nothing I buy would ever change that. It was only after I stopped buying that I actually appreciated my own unique character, me on my own, divorced from the trappings of consumerism. My frugality evolves and changes with each new iteration of my life—parenthood, homesteading, age—but it's the constant, the thread that runs through everything I do. It guides my decision-making by encouraging me to simplify, to be grateful, to never deny the abundance that surrounds me, and to recognize that there is very little I need in order to live a meaningful, fulfilled existence.

Frugality has become about far more than saving money, although that's certainly a nice fringe benefit. Alongside my spirituality and my yoga practice, frugality is how I find peace in an uncertain world and how I ensure I'm living a life I'll be proud of. I'm quite certain that no one on their deathbed has wished they worked longer hours or owned a newer car or bought more clothing. I like to imagine myself as an old woman reflecting back on a life well spent. Then, I make sure I'm creating that life and populating those future memories. Frugality removed the myopia of my perfectionism, of my fears over what other people thought of me, and my drive to meet conventional metrics of success. Thanks to frugality, I have perspective.

If Nate and I won the lottery tomorrow, we likely wouldn't change much about how we live. We'd have more money to give away to charity and we might redo our kitchen countertops (they are a weird green plastic at present . . .), but on the whole, we are content with our lives. I know that I will never be the richest, or the smartest, or the most beautiful, or the kindest, or the funniest person who has ever lived, and I am now at peace with that. I am at peace with living as I see fit and as I see best and as I want. I am happy not to spend my money trying to achieve an ephemeral state of perfection, because it'll never happen anyway. And that's not depressing to me; that's sheer liberation. Frugality mutes the noise of unnecessary desire and consumption and instead focuses us on our real priorities. Frugality opened my mind up to what I can *do* with my life, as opposed to what I can *buy*.

ACKNOWLEDGMENTS

I'm indebted to my parents, Tim and Carmen Willard; my in-laws, Rick and Debbie Thames; my siblings; and all the rest of my family for their continuous encouragement and love. I won the birth lottery and also the in-law lottery, which seems almost too lucky for one person. My parents instilled a love of reading and writing at a very young age, for which I'm enormously grateful.

Many thanks to my wonderful editor at HarperCollins, Stephanie Hitchcock, who encouraged and coaxed this book into existence through her masterful guidance and vision. Huge thanks to my agent, Sarah Smith, who adeptly shepherded me through this entire (lengthy) process. It was an honor and a delight to work with a team of such talented, dedicated, and intelligent women.

I have tremendous gratitude for all my friends who encouraged me to write this book in the first place and helped me out along the way. Thanks especially to Liz Newman for her expert advice, to Makenna Goodman for forcing me to email HarperCollins back after they asked if I wanted to write a book, to Erin Lowry for her amazingly helpful sharing of information, to Chris Goodwin for always keeping me grounded, and to Robin Junker-Boyce for her ongoing spiritual counsel and motivation to "just keep writing."

I'm only a writer because many, many people taught me how to write. Thank you to all of my teachers and college writing professors, most especially Rebecca Curtis, Adam Desnoyers, and of course, the incredible, the legendary Mary Klayder. Thanks to my bosses who pushed me every day for better writing, including Sara Garlick, Win Lenihan, and most of all Ellen Frank, who wouldn't let a single error slide past and who, in the process of our many (many) editing sessions together, became a very dear friend.

Massive thanks to my neighbor and friend Jean MacDonald (and her sidekick Alice), for her expert grandmotherly babysitting of Stella while I wrote and wrote and wrote. This book (and a whole lot else) wouldn't have happened without her presence in our lives. I'm not sure what we'd do without Miss Jean.

Thank you to the dedicated and devoted readers of Frugalwoods.com who challenge me with their questions, inspire me with their stories of overcoming financial challenges, and encourage me to keep doing what I love: espousing the liberation and joy that stem from creating a life of financial stability. I also want to express my endless appreciation for the online personal finance community, which is a source of constant inspiration, education, collaboration, and true friendship.

Deepest thanks to my very young daughter, Estelle, who mastered the art of independent play at my feet while I wrote this book. Finally, profound thanks to my husband, Nate, who kindly prodded me into this whole writing adventure in the first place. Thank you for starting Frugalwoods.com with me, for being my first and last reader, for motivating and encouraging me, and for always believing that I'm capable of much more than I realize. Thank you also for always cooking food for me and loving me with abundance.

ABOUT THE AUTHOR

ELIZABETH WILLARD THAMES is the founder of the award-winning Frugalwoods.com. At thirty-two she abandoned a successful career in the city and embraced extreme frugality to create a more meaningful, purpose-driven life and retire to a sixty-six-acre homestead in the woods of Vermont with her husband and young daughter. Started in April 2014, Frugalwoods is a respected voice in the personal finance, early retirement, and lifestyle blogging sector and empowers readers to take charge of their finances and create fulfilling lives. Thames holds BAs in political science and creative writing from the University of Kansas and an MA in public administration from American University. Prior to following her calling as a writer and homesteader, she worked for ten years in the nonprofit sector as a fund-raiser and communications manager.